Library
············and············
Information
Commission

Libraries in the Learning Community: Building Strategic Partnerships

Proceedings of an International Conference
organised by the Library and Information Commission
and Information Services, University of Sunderland
held at St. Peter's Campus
University of Sunderland
22/23 June 1998

Edited by Andrew McDonald, Vilas Edwards and Janet Stafford

**University of
Sunderland Press**

© University of Sunderland Press

ISBN 1 901888 14 2

First published 1999

Published in Great Britain by
University of Sunderland Press
The Teleport
Doxford International
Sunderland
SR3 3XA

Tel: 0191 567 4963
Fax: 0191 514 3277

British Cataloguing-in-Publications Data
A catalogue record for this book is available from the British Library

Printed in Great Britain by Athenaeum Press, Gateshead

Table of Contents

The way forward: challenges for learners, librarians and communities

Libraries in the learning community: building strategic partnerships

There is growing interest in the concept of "learning communities", and their crucial importance in the Information Society, in many countries around the world. Improving learning opportunities for people throughout their lives is high on the political agenda, and cities and regions in particular have a unique responsibility for creating and enhancing learning opportunities within their communities. Leadership, strategy, political will and collaboration are all key ingredients for creating successful learning communities.

Learning underpins successful communities in all sorts of ways. It is vital for individual quality of life, social equality and economic prosperity. It encourages creativity and development; supports democracy; promotes cultural and social values; fosters literacy; and, stimulates commercial and economic growth. Crucial as it is, learning still fails to reach many in our communities.

The libraries in our communities have long supported a wide range of learners. They are an established, trusted and accessible network of "places" which are used by millions of learners a year, often reaching those who do not have the necessary technology and resources at home or at work. The network of libraries embraces various sectors including local authorities, colleges, universities, schools, government bodies and so on.

This timely international conference was organised by the Library and Information Commission in partnership with Information Services at the University of Sunderland. It attracted a diverse audience of over one hundred senior policy makers from Government; library and information managers from the public, academic and other sectors; learning managers; and information and communications technology strategists.

The conference successfully explored a number of important themes:

- the vision of learning communities within the Information Society and the challenge of providing learning throughout life

- the central role of libraries in all sectors for facilitating and supporting lifelong learning and active citizenship

- some successful current models of library partnerships and provision in learning communities throughout the world

- how libraries must change and develop new strategic partnerships at local, regional and national levels in order to play an even more effective role in their learning communities.

Libraries are set to play a central role in the learning community agenda. In some cities, librarians from various sectors have come together to provide a comprehensive, distributed, community-based learning support service. Providing easy access to learning and information, however, requires strategic knowledge of global networks, information technology, learning support, and training in information and study skills.

The challenge for the library and information community is a considerable one. We must ensure that our distinctive contribution to providing community-wide, lifelong learning is fully understood, particularly in political circles. We must enhance our role by developing strategic partnerships between libraries in different sectors and with other key bodies involved in learning. We must extend this "ladder of learning" into our local communities. The barriers and difficulties involved in developing cross-sectoral partnerships should not be underestimated, but we must enhance the effectiveness of the network of libraries and develop powerful electronic networks in order to facilitate and support lifelong learning in our communities and retain our position at the centre of the new Learning Age.

It is fitting that a conference about partnerships should be organised through a successful partnership between the Library and Information Commission and Information Services at the University of Sunderland. We should like to acknowledge the tremendous work of the staff involved in both organisations. In particular, we should like to thank Anne Fisher, formerly of the Commission, and Vilas Edwards and Janet Stafford of the University, who have worked together so creatively and tirelessly to achieve this hugely successful conference. Thanks also to Rachel Webb of the University for coordinating the editorial work and to the University of Sunderland Press for once again publishing the proceedings of an important library conference.

Andrew McDonald, University of Sunderland
Margaret Haines, Library and Information Commission

Welcome and introduction

Dr Anne Wright CBE DL

Vice-Chancellor and Chief Executive
University of Sunderland

I am delighted to welcome you to this international conference organised by the Library and Information Commission and the University of Sunderland. I am also delighted to welcome you to St. Peter's Campus which I hope you will find an appropriate venue for the conference. The Campus has a heritage of learning as well as a heritage of industry. It is next to St. Peter's Church, the monastery where in the seventh century Benedict Biscop founded his learning community of monks, and where the Venerable Bede started as a young scholar. It is enfolded by the monastery to the north and by a sculpture on the riverside - Colin Wilbourn's sculpture 'Pathways of Knowledge', which was unveiled by Her Majesty the Queen in 1993 to inaugurate our campus here on the site of the Sunderland shipyards. The sculpture is a huge pile of stone books with an illuminated frontispiece from the Codex Amiatinas - 'In the beginning was the word...'. The sculpture is clearly visible to students reading in St. Peter's Library, a library with a serene, silent heart, the Catherine Cookson Reading Room. Dame Catherine Cookson, who died just two weeks ago, was an honorary doctor of the University and a generous donor. We named the reading room in her honour because she owed her ability to write and research her novels to her access to public libraries. She referred to her public library as the 'university for life'. She was to become one of the most extensively read and borrowed authors in this country and around the world. The counterpoint to the Dame Catherine Cookson Reading Room is the cathedral of computers across University Square in the School of Computing and Information Systems. For us, St. Peter's Campus brings together hope for the heritage of learning and learning for the new millennium, and appropriately for this conference, embodies a renaissance of learning and a renaissance of libraries here by the River Wear.

I am delighted to welcome delegates from all over the world, not only from the UK and Ireland, but also from Belgium, Finland, France, Germany, Greece, Netherlands, Norway, Singapore, Sweden and Romania. I am also pleased to welcome such a wide range of participants - senior library and IT managers from all sectors; and representatives from learned societies, education and adult learning, government, and media and communication industries.

Welcome also to our distinguished speakers - Baroness Blackstone, Minister of State for Further and Higher Education, Lord Puttnam, our Chancellor, and Matthew Evans, Chairman of the Library and Information Commission. Bob Fryer will be arriving shortly and later we will have Kate Adie and David Ruddick, and also many other figures from the public and academic library sector. A very special welcome from the University to the Library and Information Commission, with whom we have organised the conference, and particularly to its Chair, Matthew Evans, who gave the keynote address at our first international library conference two years ago on self-services. We would like to congratulate Matthew Evans on the recent award of the CBE in the Queen's Birthday Honours List. Under Matthew Evans' leadership, the Commission has produced the excellent report *"New Library: the People's Network"[1]* which has been so well received both by the library profession and by the Government, and I know that his work has now gone much further, with task groups on network development, content creation and IT training. There have also been impressive reports on research strategy and digital content creation, the later work undertaken here in the North East by Information North. These and the most recent publication on the role of libraries in the learning society, have all demonstrated that, like us, the Commission believes in developing partnerships across traditional sectors to create a learning city. We are of course also delighted that Sunderland is one of the case studies used in the Commission's research.

The University of Sunderland is involved in many successful partnerships in the City and the North East and we can claim to be moving towards the learning age. There is Learning World, the University for Industry Pilot Project, Pathways, Learning Places in the City Library and the City of Sunderland Partnership *"Telematics Strategy"[2]*. We are very proud of the close links between all the libraries in the City and in particular the Libraries Access Sunderland Scheme, which has opened up the network of libraries in the City to everyone - the public libraries, the City College learning centres and our libraries here in the University. The library card has become the key to lifelong learning for many people in the City. There is now collaborative staff training, we have looked at a shared automated system, and we have made thousands of full-text electronic journals available throughout the City. The University Library has also developed partnerships with several local organisations, including health trusts, businesses, the MEP's European Education and Information Centre, and local schools. Just a week or so ago, as part of the National Year of Reading celebration, St. Peter's Library here hosted an electronic books day for eighty local primary school children in partnership with the BBC and Blackwell's Bookshop. The large furry animals were enjoyed by school children and librarians alike. In our learning network with partner colleges in the North East, we have provided a link to the library's catalogue and other information services. In this way, the University can be a hub for a learning network in the region and a gateway to global learning and information.

The University has a sophisticated Teaching and Learning Strategy which draws together an infrastructure of libraries, learning resource centres and open access workstation laboratories to provide a high-quality learning environment for our students. We found that usage of all the learning facilities on St. Peter's Campus (particularly by the Business School and the School of Computing and Information Systems, but also by all students who come here from across the University) is extremely high, and this pays off directly in the IT and information skills of our students. In our learning innovations, here at the University of Sunderland, and off-campus in developments such as Learning World and the University for Industry Pilot, we have rediscovered the central importance of libraries as "places" which provide and support learning, "places" from which virtual services can be distributed, and "places" where librarians facilitate and support learning. We fully recognise the tremendous importance of libraries of all types for making learning available to the community and for supporting communities in their learning. Libraries are crucial to lifelong learning as a network of social "places" which are accessible and trusted by communities, and where people of all types can learn together and access a huge range of print and electronic information and global networks. From the University's point of view, libraries are crucial to our mission of community-wide lifelong learning and to our strategic vision of learning in the next millennium which we have called *'New Knowledge, New Learning'*. That is why we are so delighted to host this conference on 'Libraries in the Learning Community'.

In welcoming you to this landmark conference, I have a sense that we are on the edge of a new era of library development, with new partnerships and networks to strengthen the contribution of libraries. A renaissance for learning but also a renaissance for libraries in the new Learning Age. Now, I am particularly delighted to welcome Baroness Blackstone on her first 'live' visit to the University, and to show her the learning and library facilities at St. Peter's, although I was delighted last September also to welcome her by video conference to the Sunderland Stadium of Light for the launch of the University for Industry Pilot Project. Baroness Blackstone is Minister of State with responsibility for Further and Higher Education, and before taking up this crucial office for us all, she was Master of Birkbeck College. Personally, professionally and in Government she has a tremendous commitment to lifelong learning. Minister, we are most grateful to you for sparing the time to be with us and to give the Keynote Address. I know that the role of libraries in creating learning communities is very important to you and we look forward immensely to what you have to say. I am also delighted that the University's new Chancellor, Lord Puttnam, is here today to chair this afternoon's session and to make his own contribution to the conference. David Puttnam was installed as Chancellor and Honorary Head of the University here in the Sir Tom Cowie lecture theatre in May 1998. Chairman of Enigma Productions and producer of such films as *'Chariots of Fire'*, *'Midnight Express'*, *'Local Hero'* and *'The Killing Fields'*, David Puttnam is, of course, renowned for his lifetime of distinguished contribution to the creative industries. As a member of the Standards Task Force, he is now centrally involved in the Government's drive to ensure that all young people realise their full potential through education. This conference is Lord Puttnam's first public role in the University since his installation as our Chancellor.

Well, you have a wonderful programme, outstanding speakers and distinguished participants and I wish you an enjoyable and rewarding conference. I now invite Lord Puttnam, Chancellor of the University of Sunderland, to chair the first session and to introduce our Keynote speaker, Baroness Blackstone.

References

1. Library and Information Commission. *New library: the people's network*. London: Library and Information Commission, 1997.

2. City of Sunderland Partnership. *Telematics Strategy*. Sunderland: City of Sunderland Partnership, 1996.

The Learning Age

Baroness Blackstone

Minister of State
Department for Education and Employment

Abstract

The Government's vision for the learning society is outlined and the various initiatives put forward in *"The Learning Age"* are described. The paper focuses on the Government's plans for lifelong learning including the University for Industry and Learning Direct; investment in learning, including individual learning accounts; learning in the workplace and the role of higher and adult education.

The contribution of libraries, in particular through initiatives such as the Libraries Access Sunderland Scheme, the National Year of Reading and the Public Libraries IT Network, is emphasised as being an essential ingredient in delivering the learning agenda. Partership is recognised as being of crucial importance.

Introduction

The last time I had the pleasure of speaking to an audience in the North East, I was 'beamed in' as a virtual reality speaker over a video link. That was very successful. But I am pleased to say that today I have not been prevented by my commitments in the Lords from being here in person.

You asked me to talk about the Government's policies on lifelong learning, and to bring together all the various initiatives put forward in *"The Learning Age"*[1]. Not an easy task - nor one that I can do justice to in half an hour. However, I shall attempt to outline our vision for the learning society and to highlight for you the valuable contribution that libraries can make and are making to realising that vision.

But first, let me say a little about the European perspective. We are honoured in having our European colleagues here today. Last month, in Manchester, we hosted a European conference on lifelong learning, with delegates from all over the EU. They were discussing issues at the very heart of our own political agenda in the UK, at the heart of our Presidency of the EU - lifelong learning, employability, social inclusion and active citizenship. Making lifelong learning a reality has been an important goal in Europe. This European conference coincided neatly with our annual celebration of learning - Adult Learners' Week. If you had seen - as I did - the enthusiasm, commitment, energy and drive on display at the North West's Festival of Learning, then the importance of learning would certainly have been reinforced in your minds.

The rationale for investing in learning

Learning is the key to the future well-being of this country. It is essential to a strong economy and an inclusive society. This is at the heart of this Government's programme. Our aim is to create a fairer, more prosperous society. We want to empower all people to lead a fulfilling life. Learning does just that.

The development of skills can give people confidence and hope. They can help people overcome the barriers to work, and so open up the route out of poverty. Skilled and confident people give businesses the edge that they need to be successful in this ever more competitive world.

It is a virtuous circle. In economic terms, skilled people contribute to the success of businesses and thereby to their own prosperity. In social terms, skilled people are able to make a greater contribution to society - to feel that they have a stake in it - and society itself is thus made all the stronger.

Now this is easy enough to say but I do not underestimate the scale of the task if we are to enjoy a "learning society" and all the benefits it brings. Did you know that

70% of jobs today need cerebral skills, while 30% need manual skills? 50 years ago, the reverse was true. Or did you know that people without qualifications earn 20% less than the average wage, 25% less than those with A levels and 50% less than graduates? Almost seven million adults in the UK have no formal qualifications at all, and one in five people find reading, writing and numbers difficult?

Ladies and gentlemen, George Bernard Shaw said that poverty was "the greatest of our evils and the worst of our crimes". Poverty is not just the lack of material wealth. It is the lack of opportunity and the lack of hope. It is a waste of human potential which we cannot afford.

"The Learning Age"

Of course, poverty has to be tackled on many fronts - economic, social, housing, welfare, education - to name a few. Our Green Paper, *"The Learning Age"*, aims to tackle poverty by creating a learning society in Britain. It sets out practical proposals for achieving this vision by:

- overcoming the barriers to learning through, for example, the launch of the University for Industry

- supporting investment in learning, including through individual learning accounts

- facilitating learning in the workplace

- working with further, higher and adult education to deliver the learning society

University for Industry

First, the University for Industry - our lever for starting the cultural shift to make lifelong learning a reality. We foresee the University for Industry leading the way in transforming the learning culture in the UK - opening up access to high-quality learning opportunities to everyone and helping more people to take up learning and to learn more effectively.

The University for Industry will harness the power of developments in technology, communications and broadcasting, and it will give people the flexibility to choose how, when and where they learn - at work, at home, or in convenient local learning centres - possibly set up in libraries or shopping centres, like the partnership University for Industry Pilot led here by the University of Sunderland. I launched this Pilot - the first in the country - in September 1997 and have watched it develop as a true partnership - a partnership to benefit local people and the community. It has already obtained around 5,000 registrations for learning opportunities. Imagine the impact for the learning society once the University for Industry goes live across the country in the new millennium.

Before joining you today, I have visited Learning World in Gateshead and Pathways in Sunderland. Two places where learning is being brought direct to people - rather than making them travel to it. A trip to the Metro Centre no longer simply means a trip to Marks & Spencer or the supermarket. Now it can mean the opportunity to brush up your computer skills or to talk over your learning needs with trained staff and other learners. At the Pathways Centre, right in the heart of Sunderland, I met their 5,000th learner! And there are others all over the North East - in factories, libraries, careers services and so forth. I congratulate everyone involved in this work - your imagination and commitment are making a very real difference.

Now to return to UfI at the national level. In the autumn we expect to make the crucial appointment of the University for Industry's Chief Executive Designate. In the meantime, developments are being led by an Advisory Board, chaired by Lord David Sainsbury. This will build on the "*Pathfinder Prospectus*"[2] published earlier this year and start turning the UfI vision into a reality.

Learning Direct

A major part of the University for Industry is Learning Direct - our national telephone helpline. It provides free information and advice about learning opportunities in the UK. Anyone who has watched television or listened to the radio during May 1998 will have seen or heard the 0800 100 900 number on air. Almost four months after its launch it has taken 240,000 calls. This illustrates a real hunger for learning out there. One of the things we have learnt from our experiences of Learning Direct is the power of broadcasting in creating demand for learning. The BBC's campaign - 'Computers Don't Bite' - generated 89,000 calls in just over a week. But it is not just the BBC. The support that organisations such as libraries give by displaying leaflets and by being actively involved in Adult Learners' Week is also invaluable in generating demand for learning.

Individual learning accounts

We are introducing individual learning accounts to help people plan and save for their learning.

Look at the experience of an insurance company, the Liverpool Victoria. It is pioneering learning accounts in association with Dorset TEC. It offers £200 per account as long as employees each invest £25 of their own money and it offers everyone a £50 bonus on completion of their studies. Within three days of the scheme being announced, 30 people at just one of the company's sites had expressed interest!

I hope that some accounts will be available through TECs by spring next year, with a national system in place by April 2000. We want accounts to be widely available, through a range of banks or other financial institutions.

Our system will be built on two main principles:

- that individuals are best placed to choose what and how they want to learn

- that responsibility for investing in learning is shared

To help achieve our vision we have already announced that £150m of public money will be made available for the first million accounts. The first account-holders will have to invest a minimum amount of their own money. The Government will then support that investment, and it will be open to others, including employers, to contribute as well. Our investment in the first million accounts will provide a firm foundation for the national framework.

These first accounts will be mainly focused on those people currently in work. Within this we wish to encourage particular groups to take up learning. For example, people who have particular learning or skill needs, employees of small firms and people seeking to return to work.

The support we are offering to the first accounts will open up a wide range of opportunities. For example an initial investment of £175 made up of public funds and personal contributions could buy an introduction to word processing course, an intensive course on the Internet <u>and</u> an eight week course on accounts for small businesses at a total cost of £172, or a German business language course at £160, or City and Guilds in Electronics for £59.

Learning in the workplace

Learning accounts will be just one of the ways of stimulating demand for learning in the workplace. We want to work with businesses, employees and their trade unions to support and develop learning in the workplace. We will encourage the establishment of company learning centres with strong links to the University for Industry. We are also creating the Union Learning Fund, worth £2m this financial year. The Fund is available to all trade unions and organisations representing trade unions throughout England. It will consolidate work such as the Bargaining for Skills initiative by helping trade unions play an active, creative and supportive role in bringing lifelong learning to the workplace.

Higher and further education

But learning does not just take place in the workplace. We are working with higher and further education to create a learning society. We are committed to expanding further and higher education to provide for an extra 500,000 people by 2002.

On higher education, we have already set out new funding arrangements, building on the proposals of Lord Dearing's Committee[3], which are currently before the House of Lords. We have the 1998-9 funding package for HE, which will allow an extra £165m to be spent.

On further education, we have announced some £100m of additional funding for next year. This will provide for up to 80,000 extra students in FE, with the great majority drawn from the educationally disadvantaged population. We will consider future levels of funding for the sector very carefully through our departmental spending review.

Basic skills

But we cannot deliver the learning agenda without also investing in the foundations. I mean, of course, the basic skills of literacy and numeracy. We have set a target to double the number of adults we help to improve their basic skills to 500,000 a year by 2002. This includes many more places in further education courses, 10,000 places alone in summer schools this summer, a firm focus on the basics in the New Deal and in our plans for University for Industry, and the work of national training organisations.

The Adult and Community Learning Fund will create a partnership with trusts, charities and companies to promote community learning through innovative projects working with grassroot organisations in disadvantaged areas. We will make £15m available over the next three years and we are looking to match this with contributions from trusts, charities, companies and private donors which share the aims of the fund.

Contribution of public libraries to lifelong learning

So what does all this mean for libraries? For a start, we in Government cannot deliver the learning agenda alone. We need your help. We must not underestimate the contribution libraries are already making to lifelong learning and the potential contribution they are uniquely placed to make in the future. The City of Sunderland is pioneering library initiatives, being the first city to open its College, University and public libraries to all learners in the city.

We have recently published the National Adult Learning Survey - the first time such an extensive survey of learning, and non-learning, has been carried out. The survey highlighted the important role that libraries play in providing information - particularly to those people classed as 'non-learners'.

The public library service is one of our most widely used information and learning resources, and is also one of the most respected public services. Around 400m visits to libraries are made every year, with 10m users making a visit at least once a fortnight. Nearly 60% of adults are library members.

Let me tell you about the impact that libraries have had on people's learning. The Green Paper tells the story of Shibani Basu who was appointed as community librarian in Merton. Through the course of her work she realised that, although they brought their children, local Asian women made relatively little use of the library. Shibani knew that the library was a safe and respectable place to meet and a potentially important resource for them. And so the Asian Women's Association was set up in 1988, with membership now standing at over 250. They hold workshops, discussions, lectures, and arts and craft sessions in the afternoons rather than evenings, when the women usually have family responsibilities. Members have not only learnt a wide range of skills but some have gone on to take formal training courses. A wonderful example of how the local library played its part in creating the learning society.

The Government regards public libraries as key contributors to some of our most important policy objectives. In addition to underpinning education by providing essential support for children, students and lifelong learners, they enhance public access to the world's store of knowledge and information, they combat social exclusion by helping to bridge the gap between those who can afford access to information and those who cannot, and, increasingly, they have a role to play in the modernisation and delivery of public services. Our plans for the development of the library sector are intended to enable libraries to play an even more significant role in all these key objectives.

Initiatives such as the National Year of Reading, which will be launched in September 1998, will give libraries (along with the many others taking part) an opportunity to use their experience, ingenuity and creativity and to combine their traditional strengths with the new IT capabilities they are developing. This blending of core services and values - customer service and promotion of literacy - with new means of delivery is also central to our vision of the development of a Public Libraries IT Network as part of the National Grid for Learning.

Many of you will have read about our plans for the Library Network in the Government's response to the Library and Information Commission report, "*New Library: The People's Network*"[4]. We intend it to play a central role in delivering the Government's wider objectives for the role of information technology in society. As such, the development of the library network is an integral part of the vision of the 'Information Age' launched by the Prime Minister in April 1998 which provides the framework for ensuring that we seize the opportunities provided by new technology.

The Library and Information Commission, our co-hosts at this conference, are currently looking at how the Public Libraries IT Network can best be implemented. One thing which is clear is that its successful delivery depends on partnership, involving the private sector, local government, and library users. Government can establish the strategic framework and set the directions and pace of this process, but it cannot by itself deliver the network. To do that, we must rely on the determination, dedication and motivation we know exists within the sector. I know my colleagues in the Department for Culture, Media and Sport have been impressed by the expertise and enthusiasm already developing for the network. I am sure that it will ensure libraries continue to be a strong and vibrant link in the chain of lifelong learning.

Conclusion

In outlining our policies, I hope I have been able to convey something of our vision for the creation of a learning society. I must stress again that we in Government cannot deliver the vision alone. If we are to create a learning society we need to work with all the other players. That is why we need this national debate about the way forward for adult learning. I urge you to be part of this debate. Libraries have an important part to play both in shaping the future direction of adult learning policy and delivery. I look forward to seeing your responses to *"The Learning Age"* Green Paper.

References

1.   Department for Education and Employment (DfEE). *The Learning Age: a renaissance for a new Britain*. (Cmd 3790). London: HMSO, 1998.

2.   Department for Education and Employment et al. (DfEE et al.). *University for Industry: engaging people in learning for life*. Pathfinder Prospectus. London: DfEE, 1998.

3.   The National Committee of Inquiry into Higher Education. *Higher Education in the Learning Society*: Report of the National Committee (Chairman: Sir Ron Dearing) London: HMSO, 1997.

4.   Library and Information Commission. *New library: the people's network*. London: Library and Information Commission, 1997.

Libraries and learning

Matthew Evans CBE

Chairman, Library and Information Commission
Chairman, Faber and Faber Ltd

Abstract

The time is now right, with the advent of the Library and Information Commission and the central position of education in the policy of the Labour Government, to explore creatively the relationship between public libraries and the education system.

The need to integrate public libraries into the Government's plans for education is discussed, and obstacles to this are considered. The great challenge of future years is to educate and re-educate those who have left formal education, with libraries playing a central role, and to end the separation of libraries and education.

Over the past 150 years, the relationship between public libraries and the educational movement has been, at best, ambivalent. However, we now have an opportunity to change this relationship and to integrate our public libraries into our educational system for the greater benefit of all the citizens of our country.

The Select Committee on Public Libraries in 1849, which led to the Public Libraries Act of 1850, saw the beginnings of Britain's great public library movement. Scholars who have looked at the evidence given to the Select Committee say that it was not the educational potential of a library system that engaged people's imagination, but rather the role that libraries would play in maintaining social order and promoting moral values by providing better recreational opportunities for the urban working population. George Dawson, a non-conformist minister who played a key role in the Public Libraries Act in Birmingham, spoke of public libraries as "recreational alternatives to drunkenness, bull-baiting and dog fighting". Samuel Smiles thought the library would keep working men at home to read books away from the temptations of the world.

Two decades later, the architect of the 1870 Education Act, A. J. Mundela, said "Only through education could social mobility be established and the war of classes be brought to an end". But in his many speeches libraries did not get a single mention and were not seen as part of his great cause.

Thus, in the nineteenth century, the link which we are coming to see as obvious between the public library and education was not made explicit, and the relationship between the two was ambivalent. There was a feeling that they were part of the same vision, but there was an inability to articulate the relationship in a positive and constructive way.

Now, however, at the end of the twentieth century, we are ideally placed to explore creatively the relationship between the public library and the educational system. The time is right for two reasons: one is that the previous Government in its last year set up the Library and Information Commission to advise Government on libraries in a cross-sectoral way, including libraries in places of education. For the first time the library world had a voice close to Government. The second is that on 1 May 1997, a Labour Government was elected, and central to its policy was, and is, "education, education, education".

In a nutshell, what needs to be done is to integrate public libraries into all the Government's plans for education including, crucially, in its proposals for the National Grid for Learning, lifelong learning, the University for Industry, after-school clubs and all the other manifestations of this Government's commitment to education. We need to recognise that libraries support the specific needs of the curriculum and the more general needs of lifelong learners. Enormous progress has been made over the last year or so as, for the first time, public libraries are now talked about in Government documents relating to education. We at the Commission are doing what we can to forge permanent links. The document we published last week *"The Role of Libraries in a Learning Society"*[1] is an indication of our commitment. However, there are still obstacles to be overcome.

First of all, public libraries themselves. When I took on the job as Chairman of the Commission, I spent a great deal of time going round the country visiting all sorts of libraries and talking to all sorts of librarians. In one of our major cities I introduced the public librarian to the university librarian, both of whom had been working in the same city for a number of years but had never met. Of course, there are centres of excellence throughout Britain where the public library is outward-looking rather than inward-looking, but this was just one example of how isolated the public library service seemed to be. Cuts, year after year, a lack of vision for the service and a general lack of confidence have, I am afraid, been the norm.

A second obstacle to overcome is central Government. It is worth noting that although the public library system is the responsibility of local authorities, the statutory obligations for its superintendence and development are exercised by the Secretary of State at the Department for Culture, Media and Sport. The educational system is looked after by the DfEE. Very close co-operation between these two Government departments is needed if our common goals are to be realised.

The third obstacle is at a local level. In too many authorities, there is a real departmental distinction between education services and library services. However, some forward-looking authorities are creating learner-centred alliances in the way they structure their organisations. In Essex, for example, libraries, information, heritage and culture come together with education under a new Directorate of Learning Services. This is an example of cross-sectoral working that, with the right sort of attitude in central and local Government, will make learning a reality for everyone and engender a new age of learning and a cultural transformation for the nation. Here in Sunderland, we have an outstanding example of how the two sectors are working together.

This is my second visit to the University of Sunderland which I do think is an absolutely fabulous place. This is not only because of the situation, the buildings and the people here, but there is also something here which David Puttnam referred to right at the beginning of the session when he talked about joined-up thinking. I go to so many universities and they seem to exist for themselves and have nothing to do with what happens outside. Here, practically every cultural and artistic institution in the community seems to be linked. Interestingly, the further North you go, the more evidence you see of this happening. You see so little of this in our traditional seats of learning such as Oxford, Cambridge and even London.

Sunderland is a city renowned for partnership working and learning innovation. With Tessa Blackstone this morning, I have seen Learning World, the University for Industry Pilot Project, and the Industry Centre. The city has a Telematics Strategy too. The City Library is working closely with the City College and the University Library. Common sense you may say but it is incredible how few examples there are of this cross-sectoral activity in our country. It puts the learner and not the institution at the centre.

Learners have access to all the libraries in the city and joint staff training and electronic services underpin the service – a beacon to all sectors. I remember only last year being in another big city. In the window of the University Library, it said, "Only members of this University can enter this Library". The public library was full of students who could not find a place. I think this sort of exclusiveness has no place in the sort of vision we are talking about today and tomorrow.

Education is the right of every child in this country, but the great challenge coming up over the next few years is to educate and re-educate that majority of our population who have left schools, colleges and universities. Libraries have to be recognised as the before and after of all formal learning, offering first chances (universities for the under-fives), second chances and last chances. They are the local learning places of choice, and as this Government rolls out its ambitious plans for educating our citizens, the public library system must be central to the vision.

The separation between libraries and education, which, as I argued earlier, goes back to 1850, must be removed.

References

1.   Morrison, Marlene et al. *The role of libraries in a Learning Society*. A report presented to the Library and Information Commission. London: Library and Information Commission, 1998.

The learning challenge for the nation

Lord Puttnam of Queensgate CBE

Chancellor, University of Sunderland
Chairman, Enigma Productions Ltd

Abstract

New forms of technology are fundamentally changing the way we view the world of learning and the role and relevance of information in that world.

The convergence of moving images and the printed word, radically changing the form and nature of the information industries and of libraries is considered. A real 'learning challenge for the nation' is provided by the convergence between entertainment and education. The possibility of convergence between public libraries and public service broadcasting is raised.

Consideration is given to the relationship between education and the economy, and to the crucial role of teachers and librarians in demanding the right ICT.

One of the issues I am very keen to explore is the way in which, as we enter the new millennium, new forms of technology are fundamentally changing the manner in which we view the whole world of learning, and the role and relevance of information in that world.

I have spent 26 years or so with moving images, whilst most of you, I imagine, are primarily concerned with the printed word. But there is absolutely no doubt in my mind that our two worlds are drawing ever closer together. They are, in the jargon of our time, "converging".

This convergence, between the printed word and the technologies of television, computers and the Internet, is rapidly blurring many of the distinctions which we have traditionally taken for granted. Distinctions such as those between "printed" and "electronic" information.

As many of you know far better than I, this convergence is already radically changing the form and nature of the information industries, whether it be online guides to the libraries or the success of an online bookseller such as Amazon.com. Sitting at home in London, I can now call up computerised bibliographies from libraries around the world, and determine whether they have that key text which I just cannot lay my hands on.

The complete convergence of computers and the television set will unquestionably affect the way in which we select, borrow and purchase books. As all of you know far better than I, this has enormous consequences for any traditional concept of the library.

What is clear is that these changes are occurring at an ever-faster rate. I was particularly intrigued a few weeks ago to see that the German publishing giant Bertelsmann has announced plans to create a truly world-wide "online" bookstore, which will eventually sell titles in virtually every conceivable language, anywhere in the world. Perhaps the time when we see online libraries of this kind is not too far off either.

Of course, it is not just books and the printed word which are likely to be affected by this extraordinary transformation. Physical interaction is no longer necessary in order to trade in many, many types of goods and services, from buying the weekly groceries to investing in stocks and shares. In fact an ever-increasing amount of trade and commerce is, and will be, conducted electronically.

We will see one manifestation of that later this afternoon, when David Ruddick from the Gates Foundation makes his presentation via satellite video link.

Please do not get me wrong. I am not one of those apocalyptic future-thinkers who believes that in the twenty-first century, we will not visit the local library to borrow some books simply because we would prefer the convenience of ordering them "online".

From the very beginnings of human society, we have endlessly invented and reinvented new mediums and new technologies to enhance our ability to communicate, but at the same time, we have rarely abandoned any of our older, more established methods.

Human beings are, and always have been, social animals and communication addicts. We all realise that if you really want to get to know someone, or to discover new people or find out about new ideas, there is still no substitute for doing it face to face.

The printing press, in all of its variations, is a wonderful example of a basic technology that has stood the test of time, withstanding challenges of one kind or another from cinema, television and radio, and I am sure many more to come. But equally, I have absolutely no doubt that, in one mutation or another, it will go on flourishing well into the twenty-first century.

As I suggested a moment ago, new information and communication technologies are opening up revolutionary new possibilities for communication, for learning and even for broader aspects of our culture.

Therefore it should come as no surprise that the overwhelming dominance of the written word as our primary means of interpreting the world is rapidly being forced to give way to a more diffuse, visual, culture whose final shape is impossible to foresee accurately.

Like it or not, we are learning to live with the emergence of a new global economy fundamentally driven by two things - information and images. And these in themselves are increasingly inter-linked, as more and more of our information is conveyed through images, and in particular, through moving images.

My friend and colleague Baroness Blackstone may refer to it *as "The Learning Age"*, while others call it *"The Digital Era"*, but essentially we are all talking about the same thing.

As the distinctions between film, television, video, telecommunications and computer software start to evaporate in the face of the digital revolution, whole new industries are being created. Many of you are already moving to seize the opportunities that this is opening up, and again I am sure we will hear more about this from David Ruddick.

But, for me, far and away the most significant development of this "Information Age" is the increasing convergence between entertainment and education. When resources that have traditionally been associated with the very best in entertainment are applied to education and training, genuinely surprising results begin to flow. This is where the real learning challenge for the nation - any nation - lies.

The educational potential of the medium has long been recognised - even if not realised. In case this sounds something of an over-convenient claim, let me give you a couple of examples. In the early days of cinema, Thomas Edison predicted its primary and most valuable use would be as an educational tool. As he put it,

> *"It may seem curious, but the money end of the movies never hit me the hardest. The feature that did appeal to me about the whole thing was the educational possibilities. I had some glowing dreams about what the camera could be made to do, and ought to do, in teaching the world things it needed to know - teaching it in a more vivid, direct way".*

The way in which CD-ROMs, the Internet and other new media products are now being used in colleges, classrooms and libraries around the world suggests to me that Edison's vision is finally about to be fulfilled.

As information technology becomes more and more essential to the functioning of our education system, the need for software and support materials is going to grow, and at a truly prodigious rate.

I know something of the business skills that have made cinema the locomotive of the world's entertainment industry - and increasingly much more besides. What I have come to passionately believe is that the creative and technical skills that cinema has been learning and refining for a century, coupled with some of its business skills, should be put at the service of education, and most particularly ICT. This seems an ambition well worth fighting for.

As some of you may know, the biggest boom in the global consumer software market last year was in 'home education'. This, together with what we are unfortunately forced to call 'edutainment' generated revenues in the order of $1.5 billion. A recent Datamonitor study forecast that in Europe alone, the CD 'edutainment' market will grow by 80% in 1998, to a value of around $180m. These are beginning to be big numbers by anybody's standards.

Education and economic success now reinforce each other just as coal and steel reinforced each other in the first industrial revolution. Education is the essential fuel that increasingly drives all of the Western economies, but it now has the potential to become a unique, wealth-generating, employment-generating activity in its own right.

Learning is now widely acknowledged to be a lifelong activity, and as new communications technologies develop, good education is becoming increasingly synonymous with creative software, and much, much more.

At the most basic level, we are going to have to make sure that our universities, and indeed all our educational institutions, are equipped with the information and communications technologies which enable them to fully exploit the teaching potential of the new digital and interactive media. For, however you look at it, we have come a long way from the days when Thomas Carlyle could confidently assert that, "the true university is simply a collection of books".

Let me offer a further thought. The public library service played a major role in allowing our parents and grandparents to dramatically expand their horizons. A public library service of the twenty-first century will necessarily include an electronic library whose contents will be available on cable, or disc, or by satellite. Is this not an area in which public service television ought to find itself very actively engaged?

As the French writer André Maurois put it in a pamphlet written for UNESCO in 1961:

> *"Every library is a centre for international understanding. By its very existence, free from propaganda and prejudice and with no axe of its own to grind, the public library serves peace as well as democracy.*
>
> *Thus a public library is a real centre of culture, propagating human knowledge and dispensing delight. It is a channel for the spread of ideas and provides the members of each community with a means of making intelligent use of their leisure."*

Is that not also as incisive a description as you could wish of the true mission of any public service broadcaster worth the name?

Partnerships between libraries and public service broadcasting offer just one way of exploiting "convergence". But this whole opportunity requires us to think cross-sectorally and to encourage governments to do the same, certainly in terms of funding, but in other strategic ways too.

Both IT and networking need to be significantly expanded and developed in our public libraries, and I know that Matthew and his Commission are looking at this key priority, and in particular the crucial role of ICT training.

Here in Sunderland, major steps have already been taken to open up the libraries in the University, City College and elsewhere to everyone in the city, most particularly through the Libraries Access Sunderland Scheme - affectionately known as LASH.

But, irrespective of the technology, the real keys to success in all of this will remain teachers. Highly motivated, well-trained and well-supported teachers must be at the heart of any future strategy. Especially, since the teacher is inevitably moving from being the deliverer of learning to being the manager of learning.

And incidentally, I very much include librarians, since they too, in a very real sense, are "teachers". Not just teachers of course, but it is certainly an important part of what they do.

Whilst access to the right technology is undoubtedly a critical part of any new infrastructure, let us not forget that teachers are the most precious single element of our whole learning system. No amount of technological wizardry can, left to itself, change the performance or the opportunities of the next generation.

Whichever way you look at it, demand for ICT must ultimately be driven by the teachers. It is simply no good our imposing ICT on a top-down basis, because if teachers do not have the will and the ability to use it, then any amount of investment will quite simply be wasted.

The recent history of the learning industry in this country bears witness to the limitations of short-term thinking and the dangers of trying to skimp on resources and cut corners.

The collapse of many companies in the consumer CD market, and the recent failures of Internet-based firms such as Webmedia, should give all of us pause for thought. When it comes to the role of ICT in education we simply cannot afford to get it wrong. The economic, cultural and intellectual stakes are simply too high.

When I had the honour of being installed as Chancellor of this quite wonderful University just a few weeks ago, I spoke of my vision of what the Learning Society might really mean.

For me, it is a society in which our future prosperity, both as individuals and as a nation, rests. Not in the exploitation and manufacture of traditional raw materials, but in our education, our ability to adapt to change, and our willingness to go on developing our human skills throughout the whole of our lives.

The fusion of emerging technologies with our established skills base - in schools, colleges and libraries across the globe - into a fully accessible, user-friendly learning resource, seems to me something really worth fighting for.

That, surely, is the great learning challenge for this nation, in fact for any nation, and it is one with which all of us in this room should be proud to be identified.

Towards the Learning Age

Professor Bob Fryer

Chair of National Advisory Group
for Continuing Education and Lifelong Learning

Abstract

The author sets out the learning challenge ahead of us if we are to realise the "Learning Age". The concept of lifelong learning for all is a huge task and there is a very real danger of excluding people on the basis of age or social group. The author explains why we need lifelong learning and the importance of current initiatives in making lifelong learning "normal". It is crucially important to integrate learning into people's everyday lives and work, getting over any early fear of learning and giving people choice about where, when and how they learn.

Introduction

I have called my paper "Towards the Learning Age" because as some of you will know, I do not believe we are in the learning age. We are on the cusp of it, we have the prospect of it, we have the view of it, we have an idea of it, and we talk a great deal about it. It is a wonderful nirvana that we have heard of. When we get to this learning society, to this information age, to this Learning Age, we will all be much happier, perhaps a bit better informed, certainly more tolerant, more responsible and more active. We shall have a greater love of the arts, be more creative and maybe, indeed, be more skilful or yet more prosperous. But we do not know where this wonderful country called "The Learning Age" is. It reminds me of a couple of lads in Barnsley where I live, who got their redundancy money from the pit in the early nineties and went to the local travel agency and asked for a couple of tickets to Jeopardy. The young woman struggled to find Jeopardy on the computer. She looked again in the book and she looked around for a senior manager (but, as always, they were at a conference). She eventually remembered from her training at the local college (training in Leisure and Tourism), to inquire, to discover, to discuss, to communicate, to listen, to understand customers' needs, and she did all of those things. She said to one of the young men, "Do you mind me asking why you want to go to Jeopardy?" And he said, "I don't mind at all - we have heard that there are five thousand jobs in Jeopardy." Well it is a bit like that with the Learning Age, we have heard there is going to be something great when we get there, but we are not there yet.

I believe there is a huge agenda for the Learning Age. I cannot talk about all of these things today but I want to talk about three of them in particular. I want to talk about lifelong learning for all, why we need it and why the work that you are doing is vital for that. And then I want to talk about making learning normal and a part of everyday life, which I think is the big challenge we face.

Lifelong learning for all

First of all, lifelong learning for all. This phrase, a "culture of lifelong learning for all", is taken from the report of my Advisory Group, written in November 1997 for the Secretary of State[1]. It is what I would call a leitmotiv, a theme, a constant pattern which re-emerges in modulated form all the way through the report. It is in fact a slogan we have taken from an OECD Report of the same name, *"Lifelong learning for all"*, published a few years ago, but not the best report by any means on lifelong learning. I think the best report is undoubtedly the Delors Report[2] *"Learning: the treasure within"* and I do strongly commend it. The Delors Report offers the most wonderful vision of lifelong learning, but we took this slogan quite deliberately because we felt that this was the single largest challenge to the way we organise learning in this country. It is challenging in several ways. We are not yet talking about lifelong learning in a coherent and integrated way. There are problems at both ends of the life spectrum and the kind of work that you do should help us breach the divisions.

First of all, it is not lifelong, in the sense that a great deal of the provision, and most of the policy initiatives that we are currently engaged in, still focus too narrowly on post-16, post-school and post-compulsory provision. It is almost as if we are agnostic about what goes on in the first sixteen years of a young person's life. Yet we all know and experience it. We certainly know from research that it is in those first sixteen years that people's attitudes and aspirations, their values and their priorities, their sense of what constitutes learning and how it can fit in with their own lives, is formed and often fixed. Notice that I have not said anything about their skills and aptitudes or their achievements and qualifications in that period. I have simply talked about values, priorities, standards and outlooks. We know that young people's attitudes and aspirations are formed both from their time at school and from their wider life - in their family and community and in their consumption of the media. We know that what happens in those first 16 years is absolutely central and that is why the work that is undertaken in libraries and museums is so important.

We also know, of course, that we cannot make lifelong learning start at 16 and end somewhat embarrassingly around the age of 50. I am delighted to hear that the Secretary of State has extended the loan arrangements to 55, but that is still only a welcome beginning. Most adult men will live currently to 75 (a five-year increase in longevity in just 25 years) and women will live to 80. We already have in the population 14m people over the age of 55 and in ten years' time this will have increased by another 50%. These people bring enormous opportunities and potential resources for lifelong learning and they are too valuable to exclude from lifelong learning. We must realise that lifelong learning cannot be the preserve of education alone. It is something for health, for transport, for communication, for entertainment, for arts and culture, for family life and for the environment. All of these areas are extraordinarily important and, if we are going to achieve lifelong learning, we had better begin to think of "joining-up" our policies, transgressing the boundaries between different sorts of provision in ways that I know, for example, libraries can do.

There is another difficulty - the word all. We certainly do not yet mean all in this country. I dare say Baroness Blackstone referred to one or two aspects this afternoon. The Blunkett vision of lifelong learning is wonderfully lyrical. I guess everybody in the audience today has committed to heart David's foreword to the

Green Paper. It is so engrossing and energising that it almost wants to make you sing for joy when you read it. He defines a very broad compass of learning which shifts away from a narrow mechanistic definition of learning driven by accreditation and qualification, to a much richer and more textured notion of learning for everybody. Without question of anybody being excluded, people will find their own balance between those different objectives at different stages in their own lives, according to their own priorities and immediate circumstances. But what happens if we exclude people? This is a very serious problem. Let me just recount four simple statistics. This should stick in your mind, if not stick in your throat.

- currently we have 8m people in this country who are functionally innumerate or illiterate. To talk about the information society to these fellow adults is something of an insult.

- we have a situation where 7m of our fellow citizens have absolutely have no qualifications whatsoever. Whilst qualifications are not everything, this is a very serious situation. It is particularly serious when I tell you that the professional classes began the 1990s with a 30% chance of gaining a degree and a 7% chance of being wholly unqualified. By the end of the 1990s if you came from a professional background, you had a 60% chance of gaining a degree, a 20% chance of entering higher education, and a less than 3% chance of being wholly unqualified. If you came from an unskilled background, you started the decade with a 60% chance of being wholly unqualified and 3% chance of having a degree. Seven years later, you have a 60% chance of being wholly unqualified and a less than 1% chance of having a degree. The educational divide has widened significantly. Not only do we have 7m unqualified citizens, but within that 7m, the qualifications are also concentrated in particular social groups.

- around 35% of the same social group, social classes D and E, have serious difficulties with reading and writing and over 40% have difficulties with numeracy. These are serious deficiencies which we cannot ignore if we are to move towards a learning age.

- my final statistic is even more scary. From the little evidence we have (which is poor) around 13% enjoyed access to some form of learning at, for or through work. When the figure goes up to 13.5%, we blaze it in big headlines as a huge improvement. I am reminded of the famous dock leader, Jack Dash, when challenged about a high-percentage pay rise. He said, "Yes, I agree, but 10% of b*** all is b*** all!". This is a very serious issue because we have not yet found ways of ensuring that all people enjoy learning opportunities in, for or through work. This is a particular problem for people who work in small and medium size enterprises who are facing tremendous competition. They often work long hours and put their own lives at risk or on hold, in terms of capital investment and time with their families. This is no criticism of them but we have yet to find a way of drawing them in. I hear about wonderful schemes like Ford, Motorola and Unipart, but these are no longer typical areas of employment, particularly, may I say my Lord, in your area of expertise. 30% of the British workforce now work in companies that employ 20 staff or less.

Making learning normal

We have got to find new mechanisms, new forms of interaction, new systems of learning, new modes of engagement which are not predicated on any past forms of education activity, and which are more appropriate to todays different material and cultural circumstances. This is why this conference is so important. That is why I am so delighted to be back here in Sunderland which has been blazing the path of exploring new ways of working, such as providing learning in the shopping centre, and of using the new information and communication technologies, and of making learning something which is normal.

By "normal", I am referring to moving away from all of that fear, dread and anxiety that so many people still associate with their first experience of formal education, when all they really learnt was two things – that they were a failure and that they wanted nothing more from learning. By "normal", I also mean integrating learning into people's everyday lives, so that it connects with their family projects, their personal projects, their projects in the community, their projects with culture or creativity, their projects with work or with skills development. Making it "normal" means ensuring that people can learn where, when and how they like. The education community must become a resource to support people rather than waiting for the people to come to it. There was a famous report in 1850 to the Hebdomadal Council of the University of Oxford which said, " We are now moving from a period of élite education to mass education. It will be impossible for everybody to come to the University. Perhaps the University should go to the people." I know the Hebdomadal Council moved slowly but I somehow think that 150 years is a reasonable timetable for action.

References

1. Fryer, R.H. *Learning for the twenty-first century. First report of the National Advisory Group for Continuing Education and Lifelong Learning.* London: HMSO, 1997.

2. Delors, J. et al. *Learning: the treasure within. Report to UNESCO of the International Commission on Education for the twenty-first century presided by Jacques Delors.* London: HMSO, 1996.

The librarian in the learning community: a new vision and approach

Hilary Hammond

Acting Director of Cultural Services
Norfolk County Council

Abstract

The paper suggests that lifelong learning is now a necessity for us all, brought about by changes in demography, society and technology - such as the globalisation of work; flexible patterns of employment; skills shortages, and increased educational participation for those in post-retirement. The different learning stages are identified, from pre-school tol post-retirement with several career changes in-between. The need to "redefine work" is also discussed.

The author describes current planning stages and development in Norfolk, including work on careers guidance, literacy, learning centres, and the Information and Learning Network.

Introduction

"The Librarian in the Learning Community: A New Vision and Approach" is the topic I am going to be talking to you about. I would like to cover various points: lifelong learning stages, where we are with society and technology, and the Norfolk Information and Learning Network. I have to say that we will be looking at Sunderland to learn an awful lot from them.

Lifelong learning stages

Let us remind ourselves about the lifelong learning stages:

- pre-school

- school

- transition to work or further education

- during work

- during unemployment, for leisure or to support community activity

I was fascinated to hear Bob Fryer saying that we tend to make lifelong learning sound as if dealing with post-16 to "Oh dear, you've stopped working, you are no longer economically active, goodbye". Of course it is about a much wider range than this and it is all of this. Lifelong learning covers everything from pre-school to post-retirement. As librarians, we support the totality of this. One area that worries me is that statistic of 20% functionally illiterate people, and I wonder to what extent in my working life I have been responsible for this increase, because when I left school it was about 14%. As professionals over the last few years we have not been doing all we should have. I want to look at this area of society and the changes we have seen.

My generation expected to have one career. When I left school my careers master said to me, "Off you go, you want to be a librarian, you do understand it is a vocation? You will not earn very much, you will disappear and become a librarian for the whole of your life, and when you reach 65 you'll stop being a librarian. You will retire, put your feet up, and someone will give you a garden seat". If I were leaving school now, I would expect to have three career changes during my working lifetime (not three job changes). I would expect that my basic training and my career path would change and I would not know what I would end up doing by the time I reached retirement age. This, I think, is where the economic pressure for lifelong learning in the post-16 age is coming from.

Changes in society and technology

Another area we need to think about is the increased flexibility in employment. 70% of jobs created in the last five years are neither permanent nor full-time. 70% of jobs created, not of all jobs. Nevertheless, it is massive. We are also in a contract culture. I imagine that some of you here are working within that system. You may have a three-year contract but what do you do at the end of it? You hope that there is another contract. A high percentage of workers are self-employed. In the UK, the average weekly commitment for those in full-time work is 48 to 50 hours per week. About 15 years ago we talked of the leisure society and it is here! Either you are in work, working very, very hard indeed, or you are not in work at all. That's how the leisure society has panned out - less leisure and more work.

Even today, 25% of the working age population is economically inactive. Now that, of course, includes people who are not looking for work. Nevertheless, this is a high percentage of the working age population. As we all know, after six months of unemployment, it becomes significantly harder to find work.

The globalisation of work is a major factor even in the manufacture of baked beans. There is a factory in Kings Lynn that makes baked beans, where the staff were recently saying, "we do not like these terms and conditions that you are offering, Mr. Manager". The response was quite straightforward, "we do not have to make them here, we can make them somewhere else in the world and ship them in, it is no more expensive". An American company owns this factory in Kings Lynn. So we are talking here about a society where work goes to where people want it to be.

I have come across some interesting recent information about employee satisfaction in an RSA journal article by Carrie Cooper[1]: in the decade 1985-95, overall employee satisfaction dropped by over 11% and we are now bottom of the European listing. Job security has gone down from 70% to 48% in the same period, and again we are bottom. These statistics just reinforce the feeling of the contract culture. A quote from that article reads:

> *"developing and maintaining a 'feel good' factor at work ... is not just about bottom line factors, such as higher salaries, a penny off income tax or increased profitability; in a civilised society it should be about quality of life issues as well, like hours of work, family time, manageable workloads, control over one's career and some sense of job security."*

Now we have been looking back quite a bit so far today, and I also want to draw attention to John Ruskin, who said the same things in 1871. It worries me that these same things are still being said now, as if they are new. John Ruskin said:

> *"In order that people may be happy in their work, these things are needed: they must be fit for it; they must not do too much of it; and they must have a sense of success in it."*

Major increases in skills are going to be required. By 2000, 70% of all jobs will require college education, 35% of all jobs will require at least a first degree, but only 40% of school leavers go on to university. The natural demographic fallout is going to mean that we have a major skills gap developing.

I mentioned earlier that we were looking at the full range of lifelong learning, and I also want to look at people who have retired. These are very, very significant statistics for me and for all public libraries. In 1994/95 we started an exponential growth in educational attainment in those retiring and thus in their intellectual expectations on retirement. In 1994, 1% of those who were then retired had gone to college from school. Now I know that many, many people have undertaken short or extensive further education courses during their lifetime. In 1995, 1% of those reaching retirement age that year had gone to college. By 2000, that figure will be 7%. I think this is going to be a major factor as far as public libraries are concerned, because people's expectations of what they can do tends to increase with exposure to education during their lifetime. I am looking here at the issues as far as public libraries are concerned. We need to bear in mind that as far as universities are concerned, there is a major increase in the number of students which is over-stretching the resources of universities and causing a major problem in public libraries as well. We are looking also at a change in the way we live and operate. There has been a major shift of people into the voluntary sector. The demographic time-bomb, which we heard about so much in the 1980s and now seems to have dropped out of everybody's conversation, is still there. There is a decline in the proportion of the population of working age, and there will be a 30% increase in pensioners by the year 2025, reflecting an increase in lifespan.

"Redefining work"

RSA have been working for some time on a programme called "Redefining Work", in which the major factors are:

- customisation of output

- rise of knowledge economy

- pay for output, not for the job

- flexibility of learning

- problem solving focuses

There is the whole range of factors about what work is, how we respond to work, and how we as a society respond to what people are asking of us. William Bridges[2] reminds us that society as a whole needs to think in terms of changing the way we pay for things. Paying for output not for a job, that is, you do not receive a salary for a job, but a cheque for providing a service or producing an output. He said:

> "Whenever there is any printed list of the abilities that workers need, it always starts with reading, writing, listening, speaking, working together, leading ... the abilities people require are still the same. I would add creative problem-solving and self-knowledge, because tomorrow's worker is going to operate more like an independent small company than a traditional employee."

This change in the way that we approach our own lives and our own learning is something I think is so fundamental that I cannot emphasise it enough. Our role as librarians is to respond to that change and that is going to be extremely difficult for us to do.

Current planning stages in Norfolk

I would like to describe some of the things that Norfolk is doing to respond to these developments:

- shaping the future

- widening participation

- Norfolk Guidance Network

- Thetford on the Learning Curve

- Norwich – a Learning City

- literacy strategy

- Fakenham and Downham Market Learning Centres

- Millennium Information and Learning Network

Shaping the future is our economic strategy and Widening Participation is our response to the *"Kennedy Report"*[3]. The Norfolk Guidance Network is our response to the privatisation of the Careers Service. Thetford on the Learning Curve is one of the educational actions taken when Gillian Shepherd was the MP for Thetford in the previous Government. This was one of the very early instances where great emphasis was put on school-based learning leading into adult learning. I will be focusing on the learning centres and the Millennium Information and Learning Network in my presentation tomorrow but I'd like to finish with just a few words about learning centres now.

Information and Learning Network

We are planning 18 to 24 Information and Learning Centres. Now I am going to ask you to think about what to call these centres? They are all going to be linked electronically: some of them by fast networks and some by slower networks; some of them will be in colleges, schools or telecottages; and some of them will be in traditional buildings like this. They will all have access to learning materials, for instance, there might be a course which has been produced by a tutor which the learner follows for a number of hours and is awarded a qualification at the end. A centre will provide a video-conference enquiry service. Tutorial support is one of the things that I am very aware of - it is no good putting a learning centre in a small market town and saying to the person there, "you now have all the materials and facilities you need, but you cannot ask questions". And who should answer their questions - librarians or tutors? Or does it matter?

We have a small budget, initially only around £1.5m of which the revenue growth for the library element is only £124,000 per annum. But what are these Information and Learning Centres? At a recent planning discussion, our PR person said, "show me one". These are not buildings with masses of computers, and we are talking about small market towns in a rural county. What is it going to be like? How are you going to recognise one? How do you know whether you are talking to somebody who is qualified or not? Where are we going to find the skills for the staff who run these things? What do we advertise for? Are we looking for a teacher, for someone with educational expertise, or are we looking for a librarian, or someone with all of these skills?

It is actually quite a fascinating time, is it not, to be a 'whatever-we-are' - librarians, teachers, or whatever. Those early books, incunabula, often looked like manuscripts. Those early printers produced things that looked like the very thing they were replacing. We have a very long way to go before we can say we are beginning to deliver something that our users really will find helpful and easy to use.

References

1. Cooper, C. 1998. "The psychological implications of the changing patterns of work" *RSA Journal*. 1 (4).

2. Bridges, W. 1998. "Redefining work", *RSA Journal*, 1(4).

3. *Learning works: Widening participation in Further Education* (Chairman: Helena Kennedy, QC) Coventry: Further Education Funding Council, 1997.

The Gates library programme: training and technical support issues in US public libraries

David Ruddick

Technical Resources Institute
Gates Library Foundation

Abstract

The paper draws attention to the problems of access to computer technology and the Internet for people with lower incomes in the USA, and goes on to outline Microsoft's "Libraries Online' programme, which started in 1995. The programme has provided public libraries in impoverished areas with computers and access to the Internet.

The paper outlines the grantmaking procedures, the successes of the project, including work with children and small businesses, and the lessons learned, including the requirements of public access computing and the need for and provision of staff training.

It concludes by suggesting that libraries and library projects need to be involved in developing and furthering the use of computer technologies for a better society.

Introduction

The Gates Library Foundation was set up to address the issue of the "information have-nots". Our mission statement says:

> *"The ability to use computers and to manage digital information is becoming increasingly important for people to succeed in their education and careers. And yet, access to these technologies is sharply divided in America, largely along income lines. A child in an upper-income family is ten times more likely to have home Internet access than a child in a low-income family. Fewer than 3% of the families in the lowest quarter of income have Internet access at home, and that gap continues to widen."*

Research and experience show that there exists a whole section of the population for whom the information technology revolution is not a reality. Our lives revolve more and more around technology. Jobs require computer skills, research takes place on the Internet, high school students are applying for college via e-mail, and this affects us in numerous ways.

With that in mind Microsoft started a grant programme in 1995 called "Libraries Online!" which had as its goal to begin to address the access problem. The programme granted over $10m to 200 libraries in a variety of different sized systems in the country and in all cases the libraries chosen were in impoverished areas. In some ways this programme was an experiment to see if access to computers and the Internet could be provided in impoverished areas through public libraries. It was very successful. We found that you could bring Internet access to people who would not otherwise have it and we found that libraries were the best place to do this. Because of the success of this programme it was decided in June 1997 that the programme would be expanded, and Bill and Melinda Gates decided to put $200m dollars of their own money into the project.

The decision was made to change the grant-making procedures fairly radically. Under the new grant guidelines, we attempt to reach the poorest sections of the country in a saturation mode. Rather than provide grants to selected library systems within a state, the Library Foundation is giving state-wide grants. States who receive these grants, which vary from $2m to $5m dollars, will receive up to ten computers and an Internet connection for every library building in the state. The librarians also receive training on using computers, the Internet, and administering the computers. The idea here is to saturate the poorest areas of the country with PCs, Internet access, and to provide the librarians with enough training to serve their patrons.

Successes of the project

The first thing we learned from the 'Libraries Online!' project was that public libraries are the right place to provide access. Public libraries have staff who are used to dealing with a wide variety of the population. The one common theme for all the libraries involved in this project is the increase in usage. The increase could be seen in two main groups: young adults and the local business community. During the project we worked with a branch of the Brooklyn public library. This branch had a car park next to it where the neighbourhood kids would play basketball. They had nailed a hoop directly into the library, so for them the real use for the library was literally as a backdrop. When the computers started arriving, kids started coming inside the building. The librarians at this branch told us that not only were the kids using the computers, but while waiting their turn they were also using the print resources of the library. The other group mentioned is the local business community. In mid-sized communities there are a number of small businesses currently using the Internet in a limited fashion. Many of these business people will turn to the library for instruction on using the Internet and other software applications, and many of them will use the library's Internet access due to the speed of the connection. This becomes a very important group to have on your side when the time comes to pass new building taxes.

Lessons learned

Public access computing requires extra attention. Most software, including operating systems for PCs, is tailored towards the business community. When a new computer is installed in a business, it is generally the case that employees will each have a machine to themselves. In the public environment, up to 50 different people might touch that machine on any given day. Some of these people will have little knowledge about the use of the system, whereas others will be extremely advanced users. In many ways administering a group of public access computers is far more difficult than administering a business system. The systems that are used in a public environment must be more robust because the people who are using them are very often inexperienced and therefore have a lower tolerance of errors. They must be more robust because the educators and librarians who are administering them often have little or no previous experience. Making these systems more robust costs money. When you make that extra investment up-front, the quality of service that is offered is improved dramatically.

As an example, look very closely at the type of Internet connection you install. In the home we will typically use a dial-up connection over plain old telephone lines, and this will be sufficient for a single computer. However, a single computer placed in a library will be far better served by a dedicated leased-line connection. With a dedicated line, each new user of the computer will not have to reconnect the computer with the Internet provider and inexperienced users will not assume the computer is broken while they are waiting for it to dial in to make the connection. In general, the dedicated link will improve the overall quality of service for the end-user.

Training the librarians who have received computers has been a crucial component in the grant process. Every library that receives a grant from us will get some form of training package. There are two types of training - applications training and systems training. Applications training is a key component because the librarians dealing with the public need to be able to pass that training on to the users and be able to answer their questions. Systems training is important not only for the technicians, but also for the reference librarians as well. Understanding basic trouble-shooting techniques allows the librarian to develop a better relationship with the computer and to be in control of the computer instead of the computer being in control of them. For bigger systems we will generally fly one person to Seattle for a week-long class on building both local and wide area networks, and one person to a workshop to develop their own training materials for staff. For the smaller and mid-sized libraries we send a trainer to each building, and also host other regional training sessions. We have found that it has been very important to the librarians that a portion of their training time be spent in their own library, using the machines installed there.

For many librarians, this grant provided the first piece of technology in their library. We feel strongly that the first experience should be a positive one. Working on this project for the last few years we have come across a number of other technology grants that have not worked very well. Usually, the failed attempts will appear in the form of a cupboard filled with old circuit boards, personal computers, and CD-ROM towers collecting dust. That equipment is sitting in cupboards in various schools and libraries because at some point or another someone became frustrated enough to put it there. Some people would look at that situation and see the money that has been wasted. I look at it and see a mountain of frustration and ill-feeling toward technology that has built up. If the first experience of technology for a librarian is a negative one, then it becomes very difficult to overcome that at a later date. Finally, it is important that equipment works properly first time if you have received external funding. There is funding available from companies such as Microsoft, Cisco, Intel and the like. When they see that grants are being used successfully, they are all the more likely to continue funding further projects.

We are all well aware that there is a certain amount of fear and hesitation built up among educators and librarians alike about computing technology. Yet it cannot be denied that the computer is by far the most important information tool that has been developed in the latter half of this century. Libraries and library professionals need to be involved in developing and furthering the use of these technologies. Libraries have traditionally evened the playing field for those who wish to continue their lifelong education despite their economic situation. Library professionals should be involved in computing technology so that they may become a player in further developing those technologies to improve our society. It would be a sad situation if the information revolution were to take place without the input of information's traditional stewards.

LASHed in Sunderland:
a partnership for learning in the City

Professor Andrew McDonald

Director of Information Services
University of Sunderland

Abstract

The paper explores the unique cross-sectoral collaboration in Sunderland between the City library, the City College library (further education) and the University library, and draws attention to the significant influence of the City of Sunderland Partnership's *"Telematics Strategy"*, showing how it contributes to the development of Sunderland as a "Learning City".

The Libraries Access Sunderland Scheme is discussed, outlining the way it was set up, its many benefits, the way it was promoted, and progress and developments, including staff training; joint research projects; sharing catalogues; city-wide electronic journal provision; and supporting learning innovation.

The paper highlights the importance of libraries in lifelong learning and their place in creating learning cities, drawing attention to the challenge facing the library community in developing new networks and partnerships for learning.

Sunderland - the Learning City

The libraries in Sunderland are working closely together to support community-wide, lifelong learning in the City. This unique, cross-sectoral collaboration between the City Library, City College Library (further education) and the University Library, distinguishes Sunderland as a Learning City and is but one example of the many successful partnerships for which the city has become renowned.

All three institutions are committed to lifelong learning and to encouraging wider participation in learning in the broadest sense, in a city with one of the lowest participation rates in further and higher education in the country. We recognise that improving learning opportunities and skills training within the community as a whole is an important contribution to social and economic regeneration of the city.

Another significant influence has been the City of Sunderland Partnership's *"Telematics Strategy"[1]* launched in 1996. Drawn up by local government, academia, business and the voluntary sector, it is a strategy to establish Sunderland at the forefront of telematics nationally and internationally, and to ensure that everyone in the city benefits from developments in the use of computers and telecommunications. Engaging the voluntary sector has been extremely valuable since they have a particular understanding of the real needs of people in the city, and this may sometimes be different from the view of the institutions involved. The Strategy concentrates on three main themes: the intelligent city; education and training; and business. Enhancing access to library and information services throughout the city was a key objective within the intelligent city theme. Through a city-wide network, the ambition was to link online catalogues and enhance access to electronic information sources. Already, novel Learning Places had been established in the city libraries where the public could access electronic information and IT facilities and be trained in their use.

I should like to mention two University-led initiatives for delivering "lifestyle" learning throughout the community which in the last two years have encouraged almost 10,000 people back into learning. Meeting the library and information needs of these new lifelong learners is a significant challenge for us all.

Learning World is a joint venture with Gateshead College providing a friendly, accessible and different kind of learning experience in the Metro Centre, Europe's largest shopping mall. Open at weekends and in the evenings, it is based near where people work (6,000 employees), shop (26m visitors a year) and live. Learning World has recruited about 4,000 new learners in the last two years onto business, computing, health and language courses, from basic to master's levels.

The University for Industry Pilot Project, co-ordinated by the University and the Institute for Public Policy Research, has also attracted over 5,000 new learners in just ten months in the North East. UfI is really a simple concept but it is important to grasp that it is not a new university and is not really just for industry, although learning at work will become increasingly important. Essentially, it is a one-stop-shop for education and training, a gateway to existing lifelong learning opportunities. By calling a freephone number, people have easy access to information, advice and enrolment for a whole range of courses. It operates 12 hours a day, 7 days a week. Staff at the call centre search our Internet database for suitable courses from a number of providers, including the University, a number of local further education colleges, the National Extension College, TECs in the region, the BBC and local companies. The courses can be studied at one of the 47 UfI learning centres around the region situated in places to suit people's lifestyle - in companies such as Vaux, in stores such as Sainsbury's, in health centres, in factories, in the Football Club's Stadium of Light, and in libraries.

The success of the Pilot Project has indicated the huge potential of the UfI to make a real difference to lifelong learning when it is rolled out nationally. May I mention two very interesting features. Cold telephone calling has resulted in a staggering 22% success rate in enrolment, and the analysis of demand for learning by postcode gives us the potential to respond to local requirements or even commission new courses.

Libraries Access Sunderland Scheme

This innovative, open access library scheme was launched in July 1997, and it promotes access to the wealth of libraries and learning resources in the City of Sunderland. Affectionately known as LASH, the Libraries Access Sunderland Scheme was planned by the City Library and Arts Centre, and the libraries of City of Sunderland College and the University of Sunderland. It is a fine example of cross-sectoral collaboration, or partnership between the public, further education and higher education libraries.

Under the Scheme, anyone who lives, works or studies in Sunderland has free access to all 29 libraries in the City. This includes the 21 public libraries, the four learning centres in the City College and the four libraries in the University. Learners can study at any of the 3,000 reader places in these libraries spread around the City and they can make use of the collections and services provided there. All the user needs is a current membership card for Sunderland City Libraries or a current library card for the City College or University. Users are simply asked to respect the regulations of the library they are using and study in a responsible way with consideration for the needs of other learners.

The benefits

In our view, promoting access to the network of libraries in the City encourages learners of all ages in our community to step on the *ladder of learning*. Providing seamless access between libraries also enables learners to progress on this *ladder of learning* and develop their interests without unnecessary institutional barriers. It is an important building block of the City Partnership's *"Telematics Strategy"* and an attribute distinguishing Sunderland as a Learning City.

We believe the Scheme has numerous benefits:

- it opens up the world of learning to the people of all ages in the City

- learners can use the whole range of libraries in the city, not only the City Library but also the College and University libraries

- people have somewhere to study and learn with free access to books, IT and services

- learners can use the nearest or most convenient library, and this may be particularly attractive to part-time and disadvantaged students

- the public are encouraged to use academic libraries

- members of the public may get their first taste of life on campus

- registered staff and students of the City College and University have reciprocal access rights for the first time

- the academic institutions are reminded of the value of the public library

- the public have access to information about courses, training and learning opportunities in the City

- sharing resources means that everyone can benefit from the investment in libraries in the City

How did we do it?

A small working group drawn from the three institutions came together with a clear commitment to develop a scheme which had learners rather than institutions or libraries at its heart. In addition to the Head of Library Services in the City Library and Arts Centre, the City College and the University, we also had the Vice Principal of the City College, the IT Development Officer of the City Library and Arts Centre and, usefully, the Head of Adult Education in the City.

Our focus was simply to open up our libraries to everyone in the city. We carefully considered the opportunities and implications of an open access library scheme both for learners in the city and the libraries and institutions concerned. We aimed to minimise bureaucracy and to share any costs involved.

Determined to make progress on what we fully appreciated was a challenging task, we firstly decided to identify all the positive benefits and potential of the Scheme, and we then went on to list our various concerns. These included:

- possible competition for study places, collections and IT especially at busy times

- the need to restrict the use of certain collections and services, such as the student text collections in the academic libraries

- how to enforce the rules and regulations of each library

- responsibility for damage, loss or bad behaviour

- the security of the buildings, collections, computers and people

- informing new users of health and safety regulations

- the risk of and responsibility for admitting very young people

- the difficulty if the library is in another building to which access cannot be granted

- we thought the public might need a helpline in each library

The working group considered each of these concerns and resolved them satisfactorily. For example, it was accepted that responsibility for dealing with cases of damage, loss or bad behaviour should lie with the host institution and that enrolled students should come first in the academic libraries. We were unanimous that the benefits heavily outweighed the perceived difficulties and that the Scheme had tremendous potential to enhance library and learning support throughout the City.

Even at that early stage we identified a number of interesting possible future developments but because they all required further discussion and organisation, we decided to defer them and go ahead and launch the simple access scheme.

Promotion

The Scheme was actively promoted throughout the city and learners have been positively encouraged to use all the libraries in Sunderland. This is perhaps one feature that distinguishes us from other cities in which public access to academic libraries is offered "in principle" or at least whilst there was a requirement to do so under the now defunct Net Book Agreement.

An attractive, professionally designed bookmark advertises the Scheme and gives some clear messages - *"our libraries are open to everyone", "Sunderland - The Learning City"* and *"lifelong learning - all you need is a library card"*. A colourful leaflet gives further details of how the Scheme works and information about all the libraries in the city. The Scheme was promoted in the local press and through displays in the libraries, adult education classes and various local interest groups. It was also advertised on our Web site on the Sunderland Host.

Progress and developments

Since the Scheme was launched in mid 1997 we have, together, made considerable progress on a number of fronts, including joint staff training and development; sharing online catalogues; delivering electronic journals; supporting certain learning initiatives; and undertaking research projects.

Staff training

We have encouraged joint staff training, not only to share the benefits, but also to promote an understanding of the collections and services in each of the libraries in the city. Well-informed staff throughout our libraries are important in underpinning an effective scheme. The senior management teams, middle managers and library assistants from the three library systems have all held joint training and development events. In most cases this has been the first time staff from different libraries in the city have ever met and certainly the first time they have visited each other's libraries. As well as providing an opportunity for an exchange of experience, useful ideas have emerged, particularly, it has to be said, from the library assistants. A Web site has been designed and LASH packs have been put together which give details of the services in each library. The chief librarians of the City Library and the City College have been invited to the University Library staff conference.

Sharing catalogues

It has proved difficult to share our online catalogues because we all have different systems at various stages of development. The University's online catalogue has been made available at the central public library and is, of course, available on the Internet. We would like to pursue broadcast searching or some sort of catalogue clump. A consultant is investigating the advantages, costs and savings of adopting the Ameritech (Dynix) system currently used by the University Library in all the libraries in the City.

Electronic journals

An exciting development has been making several thousand full-text electronic journals available throughout the city's libraries on Internet terminals. The three libraries have jointly negotiated a city-wide licence with EBSCO for their Masterfile service. The journals are just at the right level to be of interest to the public and users of the further and higher education libraries, and the new service has attracted considerable interest from the business community and other groups. We understand this city-wide licence is the first of its type in the UK.

Learning innovation

Because of our close links, the libraries in the city have been able to respond quickly to learning innovations. For example, they have all been designated UfI Learning Centres as part of the University's Pilot Project. Indeed, it is no surprise to us that the public libraries have proved to be amongst the most popular learning centres with these new lifelong learners.

Research

The University, together with its partners in the city, has successfully bid for a British Library Research and Innovation Centre research grant to investigate the staff training necessary to underpin successful local library collaboration and service development.

Outcomes

In our experience many of the predicted difficulties about cross-sectoral library collaboration which, it has to be said, mainly seem to arise from those who have not tried it, have turned out to be unfounded. None of the three libraries have been overwhelmed by new users and those we have attracted have not presented us with any major difficulties. The only reported problem so far has been University students making increased use of the free interlibrary loans service at the public library when their free allowance in the University has been used up. The costs have been minimal. We have simply shared the modest costs of publicity and subsequently the cost of the subscription to the EBSCO Masterfile service. The considerable benefits and huge potential of the Scheme far outweigh any minor difficulties and costs.

We have not yet undertaken any systematic evaluation of the uptake or benefits of the Scheme not least because we are aware there would be certain costs involved. However, anecdotal evidence suggests that women returners are now making greater use of the University's libraries, and this is just the sort of group whom we thought might appreciate the use of a high-quality learning environment and whom we welcome into higher education.

It is reassuring that the achievements of the libraries in the city are regarded as one of the most successful aspects of the City Partnership's *"Telematics Strategy"*. As a result, the librarians of all three institutions are now closely involved in planning the next five-year *"Telematics Strategy"* for the City of Sunderland and this will revolve around three main themes: business and industry; the digital citizen; and education and training.

LASH has attracted considerable interest in the profession and this has been a welcome endorsement of our brave efforts in developing the Scheme. There is a certain pride in the city and its libraries in the Scheme. On the other hand, we fully recognise that this sort of open access policy may not be high on agenda for libraries in other cities, although it may well be appreciated by the learners themselves.

Our plans

We intend to extend our successful joint staff training and development programme, and to investigate further city-wide licences to electronic information and to even consider collaborative purchases. In view of the interest of the business community in city-wide electronic information services, we would like to explore similar services for the health, legal and community information sectors. We would very much like to hear from vendors with relevant products, particularly full-text services.

We have discussed the feasibility of a city-wide document delivery service using manual and electronic means, believing it to be easier to lend to each other than for the academic libraries to lend to the public. We have even discussed using our minibuses to transport readers and, more realistically, books around the city.

A common library card might be attractive but, in a way, we already have this with the City Library card. For the moment, it is easier to have the particular cards necessary for the different issue systems in all three libraries, but the introduction of a city smart card might make us think again.

We would like to make more course and careers information available in each library and enable users to enrol directly on to courses whilst they are in the libraries.

Other libraries in the surrounding areas in the North East Region are interested in joining our Scheme for access and electronic services. We would also like to involve the schools in Sunderland, particularly as progress is made in connecting them up as part of the National Grid for Learning. At a time when the concept of a "learning centre" is broadening, we wonder how we can involve the electronic village halls and the UfI Learning Centres in the region.

There is tremendous scope for delivering ICT training locally and for developing digital content and local archives with the resources made available as a result of *"New Library: The People's Network"*[2].

We would like to evaluate the Scheme and, in particular, collect some statistics about who is using our libraries, and assess the benefits to them and our institutions. It would be interesting to find out how many people have been encouraged to use the academic libraries and enrol on courses as a result of the Scheme. Indeed, the Scheme could prove to be a powerful recruitment tool for the academic institutions. Similarly, the City Library would like to know about the take-up of local authority courses as result of publicity in the libraries. Further research might consider the economics of cross-sectoral partnerships, and the service standards or the explicit service entitlement of lifelong learners in the city, and could identify some performance indicators against which a Learning City might be assessed.

It is worth mentioning some other partnerships achieved within the City. The University Library, for example, has collaborative relationships with a number of health trusts, Learning World, the European Education & Information Centre at the MEP's Office, the UfI Pilot Project, some local schools, electronic village halls, the new National Glass Centre, the BBC and Blackwell's Bookshops. It is important that we look beyond building strategic partnerships with libraries and collaborate with the other organisations involved in learning in both the public and private sector.

Some lessons and observations

Many librarians suggest that cross-sectoral collaboration and an open door policy can be both expensive and problematic, and are particularly concerned about being overwhelmed by new readers. In our experience this is not the case. Indeed, it seems that many librarians overestimate the problems involved, and it continues to surprise us that many of the enquiries we receive about the Scheme focus on the problems rather than the benefits. Whilst it is true to say that the planning group itself identified a number of potential problems, we only did this *after* considering the benefits of the Scheme, and none of these perceived problems have caused us any difficulty in practice.

Our approach has been pragmatic and very much along the "just do it" lines. We were careful to introduce a simple scheme which we could communicate and deliver immediately rather than attempt an elaborate scheme which might be ultimately self-defeating. For example, our discussions about introducing borrowing raised a number of difficulties and so we decided to introduce the simple access scheme without it. In any case, we were not at all sure about the real demand for borrowing and whether a city-wide document delivery system might be preferable. We have chosen to introduce new services and developments as we have gone along. Our clear focus has always been upon the needs of the learner in the city rather than the particular interests or idiosyncrasies of our libraries and institutions.

This is not to say that "joined-up" cross-sectoral thinking is not challenging or without difficulty or even disagreement. We all have preconceived ideas which often arise from prevalent attitudes and funding arrangements in our particular sector. I was reminded when we were planning publicity material just how misleading and even threatening the term academic library could be to certain members of the public.

We believe that successful cross-sectoral collaboration is underpinned by effective "human networking" amongst the librarians in the city. A number of factors have contributed to our progress: a culture of co-operation rather than competition in the city; the political will in our institutions for lifelong learning; the framework provided by the *"Telematics Strategy"*; the lack of any significant costs; good co-operative attitudes amongst the library managers and staff; and effective communication between the libraries. There may be a greater feeling of competitiveness in cities where there is more than one of a particular type of institution. In Sunderland, we are fortunate to have just one university, one further education college and one public library. As with many new developments, there was a need for a catalyst or someone to take a leading role.

Indeed, the Scheme has generated considerable enthusiasm in many quarters of the city. Even those designing the publicity material grasped the concept enthusiastically and were pleased to be involved in a simple but cutting-edge development.

Conclusion

As I have described, the libraries in Sunderland have worked together across traditional sectoral boundaries to create a unique, open access library scheme which is playing a significant role in facilitating and supporting community-wide, lifelong learning within the city. The Libraries Access Sunderland Scheme is an important achievement and one which distinguishes Sunderland as a Learning City.

It is not common for university, further education and public libraries to work closely together in this way, and we understand that LASH is amongst the first, if not the first, cross-sectoral, open access scheme of its type in the UK. However, our work has gone well beyond actively promoting broader access. Jointly, we have introduced several new services, including electronic information services and support for new learning initiatives, and have developed collaborative staff training and research projects. This "joined-up" thinking in the library community in the city is just another example of partnership working for which Sunderland has become justifiably renowned.

As a nation, we are lurching towards a rather different education system with an emphasis on mass further and higher education and lifelong learning, and one which will be led more by customer needs than by the interests of traditional providers. Lifelong learners really do exist and we must find ways of supporting this new learning which will not only be delivered in educational institutions, but will also, increasingly, be delivered to the home, to communities, to the workplace, and to learning centres in all sorts of places convenient for people's lifestyles.

The challenge for library and information services is how we can respond to these changes. As our experience in Sunderland indicates, we must develop a system with learners rather than libraries and parent institutions at the centre. We must think across traditional sectors and develop partnerships between libraries and other bodies in order to deliver a network of learning opportunities to people when, where and how they need it. We need human and electronic networking. We need "joined-up" thinking. As the *Declaration* from the Library and Information Community published by the Library Association[3] in 1998 so beautifully put it:

> *"The Library and Information Community will break down barriers and create the new alliances necessary to realise the vision of a Learning Society and attain the objectives of the National Grid for Learning and the People's Network"*

If we fail to grasp the nettle and deliver the support required in the New Learning Age, other organisations are well-placed to do so - the BBC and Microsoft to name but two. We can speculate where resources may be invested or redirected in the Learning Age, but higher education should not underestimate the importance of further education and no one should underestimate the importance of schools and public libraries in delivering the Government's agenda for lifelong learning. There were some poignant messages for higher education from Kim Howells, the Minister for Lifelong Learning, when he addressed a recent SCONUL meeting. He likened libraries to "lighthouses" or "beacons of learning" and spoke of "fortress higher education".

There seem to be several barriers to greater collaboration and partnership working in the library world: the funding, politics and culture of the various sectors; institutional competitiveness; and inequalities in funding. Indeed, some librarians receive little encouragement to develop strategic partnerships and certainly do not receive any additional resources in order to promote new cross-sectoral initiatives. They often refer to poor vision and direction at institutional level. However, in some cases it may be the attitudes of librarians themselves which are the barrier to change. Developing partnerships need not be a costly exercise and the allocation of library resources is always a matter of priorities. What is clear is that the learner in any city can face a bewildering range of libraries and some formidable barriers to gaining access to the library and information services necessary to support their learning.

There is a great deal of investment in building digital databases at the moment but it would be a tragedy if the learners in our communities could not have access to this information, either because it is locked up in selected academic and research libraries or because of prohibitive licensing costs or restrictive copyright legislation.

It is regrettable that the contribution of libraries to lifelong learning continues to be underestimated in some circles. Many learning cities are planned without taking the crucial role of libraries into account. Several conferences on learning cities in recent years have failed to address the importance of libraries in distributing and supporting learning in the communities they serve.

However, I believe there is a tremendous future for libraries in the Information Age. Indeed, The Learning Age could lead to the rediscovery or a renaissance of libraries. The various libraries in any city or community form an accessible, trusted network of places where learners can study, access information of all types, use IT and benefit from the support of trained information professionals. Libraries also form the hub for distributing networked electronic or virtual services to the community. Our experience with Learning World and UfI confirms the central importance of libraries in supporting innovation in the delivery of learning. The network of libraries is used by millions of people a year and already makes a tremendous contribution to community-wide, lifelong learning. Our contribution could be enhanced by developing new strategic partnerships with other libraries and with the other organisations involved in learning.

In Sunderland, we can claim to have "joined-up thinking". The libraries in all sectors are working together and LASH is playing a significant role in facilitating and supporting community-wide, lifelong learning. The City recognises that libraries are a crucial element in the development of a successful learning community. As our promotion bookmark proudly proclaims, in Sunderland

> *"our libraries are open to everyone"*
> *"libraries for lifelong learning - all you need is a library card".*

References

1. City of Sunderland Partnership. *Telematics Strategy.* City of Sunderland Partnership. Sunderland: 1996.

2. Library and Information Commission. *New library: the people's network.* London: Library and Information Commission, 1997.

3. The Library Association et al. *A Declaration from the Library and Information Community.* London: The Library Association, 1998.

Towards the lifelong library: experiences from Birmingham

John Dolan

Head of Central Library
Birmingham

Abstract

This paper reviews strategic principles and opportunities, and looks at the learning environment, the learner and the changing face of learning, offering an insight from the experience of Birmingham Library Services.

It examines the vision of *"New Library: the People's Network"*, in particular the priority areas of lifelong learning and regional aspects of access to opportunities, drawing attention to the importance of cross-sectoral collaboration, re-training of library staff, the National Grid for Learning and University for Industry, and participation in the community. The need to restructure funding, especially in relation to the purchase of electronic information, is highlighted.

The experience of Birmingham is examined, starting with the environment, culture and needs of the lifelong learner and going on to look at some of the initiatives developed in Birmingham to meet them

Introduction

I am going to tell you a little bit about some experiences at Birmingham. I wish to approach this from the context of *"New Library: The People's Network"*[1], the report produced last year on public library networking. I want to start with the national picture and move on to Birmingham to see how the two relate.

It is just over a year since the Library and Information Commission produced a public library networking plan, and just under a year since the Commission handed over to the Government its report on that plan, *"New Library: The People's Network"*. This has been widely acclaimed and extensively discussed.

This presentation reviews the strategic principles and opportunities, looks at the learning environment, the learner, and the changing face of learning, and offers an insight into the experience from Birmingham Library Services in this period of rapid and dramatic change.

A renewed library service was the vision of *"New Library: The People's Network"* - refreshed, redirected, up-to-date services meeting the country's needs for the new millennium. This would be delivered by newly-skilled, re-trained staff through a UK-wide infrastructure with agreed standards for quality, service and accessibility. The library service could be a key platform for the delivery of the new Government's strategic policy objectives of economic prosperity built on social inclusion and a caring society of self-supporting, self-confident communities and people. *"New Library: The People's Network"* highlighted a number of areas as priorities for the content and services which should be delivered through public libraries in order to realise those strategic policy objectives. The two that have subsequently emerged as having overarching strength are lifelong learning and those related to a modernised, inclusive local, regional and national government. The other parallel strand to lifelong learning, one that has emerged as a key priority for the future is reflected in what Professor McDonald has just addressed, and that is the regional dimension for government, citizenship and for access to opportunities. An essential part of the concept (and Andrew McDonald touched on the importance of cross-sectoral collaboration in training) is the re-training of library staff at all levels to deliver new services in new ways. The significant issue is, and will be, the capacity of library staff to undertake new or diverse roles and create a library resource which will be a focal point for community access and learning, to become a more pro-active provider, almost a teacher, definitely a facilitator, for people who do not have access otherwise to new learning opportunities and resources.

So where are we now? You will be familiar with some of the progress that has taken place. There have been a whole raft of reports, not least the Green Paper on

Lifelong Learning, and the Government's paper *"Our Information Age"*[2], the response delivered by Tony Blair at Croydon Library. It has been an unprecedented achievement to have the Prime Minister in a public library launching a national strategy - a tremendous opportunity for us to build on. The National Grid for Learning emerged over the last year or two in parallel with *"New Library: The People's Network"*, and the two have been closely tied together. The University for Industry is a further opportunity for the delivery of learning opportunities to people in all sorts of places from all sorts of backgrounds and with all sorts of needs. From the library manager's point of view, the Government has earmarked a total of £70m from the new lottery fund - £50m to develop content and £20m for library staff training. There are two groups working on the guidelines for how that funding should be allocated when it becomes available next year and the third group is looking at the infrastructure specification, to complete the picture of the public library network in the UK. At the moment there is £6m from DCMS/Wolfson and hopefully more to follow in the future.

It is very difficult sometimes to recall how much has happened in the last 12 months in terms of the shift in Government policy and the opportunities that have arisen from both research and strategic reports for the future development of various services, and just how much has happened to bring those two together and to demonstrate the proximity between public libraries, other partner services and Government policy. The priorities that come through again and again are education and lifelong learning relating to employment.

The whole issue of Best Value and modernising local government is the other parallel strand and all these initiatives have the ultimate objective of economic prosperity based on social inclusion. In making the change for libraries we are now looking at transition areas. This will make considerable demands in terms of the library and its users, and also current non-users, who are hopefully going to discover the library of the future. This will necessitate a new staff-user interface, a new empathy and accord between people which will hopefully bring staff out from behind the counter, as at Birmingham, to give a direct and proactive support to users. I do not want to be complacent about this. Kevin Harris is at the conference and you will recall that also last year *"The net result"*[3] was published, a report looking at social inclusion in the information age, taking the view that while libraries were ideal points for community communications they, nonetheless, fell short of providing the complete opportunity. I recall the report said that libraries are in the community but are not always of the community, referring again to the transition for the library and its relationship with the community.

Lastly, a new interface with resources. We have just heard about some of the restrictions on access to certain electronic resources in the higher education domain.

A new concept is required around the creation and purchase of electronic information. It requires a restructuring of funding to promote convergence and to turn the library into a responsive and creative organisation - Sunderland is a wonderful example.

In Birmingham, my experience is that firstly, we have to go out and face the environment which the lifelong learner is inhabiting. That person or citizen is learning for a new industrial era. The whole impact of technology, communications and world trade on the back of an international information economy is not just something that hits people in businesses or industries or services, but will impact on every citizen. The learner is learning for a new industrial era, for a new economy and a new kind of democracy. That learner is going to have to pick up core skills, not just the old literacies but the new literacies - information skills, visual skills, imagination skills and design skills. To benefit from the greater opportunities that this prosperous economy, this inclusive community will offer, the learner is going to have to become articulate, able, involved in his or her community's culture, citizenship and communication structures. So, the "new learner" that I am beginning to anticipate, is somebody who has a new kind of self-perception and a new kind of motivation; someone who has discovered a reason for wanting to learn outside the compulsive or restricted formal education environment; somebody who is coming to learning at a different age, a different time in life, from a different background, and with different previous experience.

The Radio 4 programme, *In Business*, recently looked at lifelong learning and the business environment. Somebody referred to the need to give people a "self-employed culture", an environment that is full of opportunities in which they can nonetheless act independently, because sometimes it can be an isolating and competitive environment. The learner is coming with an awareness of those opportunities, with a need for access to information and guidance, responding to changing pressures and demands and the changing mix of needs and expectations. Therefore, in order to realise the needs of that learner, we have to develop new kinds of learning. We need to shift from campus-based teaching to community-based learning and from a closed education environment to a much more open landscape. In developing new kinds of learning, we need to overcome traditional constraints of location, age, eligibility and accreditation. These cannot be solved immediately. These are the things that we have yet to address.

We should remember that there are still other issues around at the moment. *"New Library: The People's Network"* is very much a focus for our attention but there are other dimensions to learning, other dimensions to the future of librarianship which we have to draw into the debate. Otherwise it will be incomplete. Another recent report, *"Public Libraries, Ethnic Diversity and Citizenship"*[4] is a piece of national research funded by the British Library, and has highlighted the institutional racism of the public library service in the UK. You cannot have social inclusion if you only get 35 senior managers from the 27,000 people in public libraries going to a launch of such a document.

Now to some of the schemes and projects in Birmingham. Like Andrew McDonald's initiatives in Sunderland, we have a number of developments in Birmingham which are collaborative and, indeed, linked to each other.

- "Futures Together" is a British Library-funded research project looking at networking in relation to unique and special collections across different library sectors. As well as information on resources it will also address access policies which put the learner before the institution.

- "Stories from the Web" (also British Library-funded) will introduce children to the Internet through creative literature and reading. It involves Leeds and Bristol libraries, and authors and publishers too.

- "Training the Future" is a partnership with Shropshire Libraries to explore the training needs of library staff anticipating new roles in the networked environment.

- "ASSIST" is the City's own Web site development. As the lead service, Library Services are negotiating partnerships with diverse contributors including City Council departments and organisations in the private and voluntary sectors.

The point of listing those examples is twofold. Firstly, all of them involve collaborative working with library and non-library organisations. This has become a central feature of any development activity in recent times. Secondly, they all involve external funding or financial or in-kind contributions from partners. Recycling local budgets, matching partners' contributions, bidding for external funding are distinct features of service development activity which have come to the fore in the last decade or so. External and partnership funding is no longer an occasional matter; it is essential to most new projects. As such, it creates new expectations of library managers, and requires new skills and approaches if we are to be innovative successfully.

In the electronic age in particular, collaboration has become intrinsic to our operation and management. There is no point in networking unless you are networking with someone else. Furthermore, such is the cost of this kind of development that it cannot be sustained by mainstream budgets.

In the world of education and learning we must replace competition with openness. We need to develop policies and strategies which are convergent. This is a matter of unprecedented cultural and organisational change. The future "New Library" beckons, but it demands that we change how we think, plan and operate. We are truly moving into an era of communication and collaboration.

References

1. Library and Information Commission. *New library: the people's network*. London: Library and Information Commission, 1997.

2. Department for Trade and Industry (DTI) *Our Information Age: The Government's vision*. London: DTI, 1998.

3. National Working Party on Social Inclusion. *The net result: social inclusion in the Information Society. Report of the National Working Party on Social Inclusion. (INSINC)*. IBM UK and Community Development Foundation.

4. Roach, P and Morrison, M. *Public libraries, ethnic diversity and citizenship*. British Library Research and Innovation Centre: Report 76. London: British Library, 1998.

INSPIRE: the virtual library network of Indiana

Millard F Johnson

Executive Director
Indiana Cooperative Library Services Authority (INCOLSA)
Indiana, US

Abstract

This paper reports on the development of INSPIRE, Indiana's first implementation of the concept of the virtual library network. It discusses the vision of the role of libraries in the 21st century, the role of the library network in helping libraries fulfil that vision and the partnership among libraries and their organisations. It describes how a consensus approach to achieving the virtual library network was achieved, the strategy by which funding was sought, and, finally, the steps in building the system.

Background

By the mid-1990s, it was clear that the explosive growth of the Internet and people's acceptance of information delivered electronically would have profound effects on libraries of all types. It was not, however, clear what that effect would be, nor what a library's response to the new technology should be. "The Information Age" is the term used by futurists to describe the escalating acceptance of the electronic information medium. These prognosticators see a social revolution as we move to "The Information Age" as profound as the revolution experienced when society moved from "The Agricultural Age" to "The Industrial Age". The new revolution could see shifts in economic prosperity and social disruption equally as great as those associated with the industrial revolution. Libraries, as society's public information institutions, ought to play a central role in "The Information Age" but, pressed by a trend of fiscal conservatism against funding growth in public institutions, libraries had experienced increasing difficulty even maintaining traditional print-based services, much less developing new electronic services. In response to the advent of the electronic information revolution, the Benton Foundation[1], in a report funded by the Kellogg Foundation, conducted a study of America's attitude to library services in the electronic age. The report showed little consistency of response. Anything was possible. Responses ranged from: libraries are no longer needed in the electronic age (they should be funded by voluntary contributions and staffed by retired volunteers) to patrons would be willing to pay $30 per month to have libraries deliver information to them in electronic form. One rational conclusion that can be drawn from the Benton Report is that libraries can have a significant role in determining their destiny in the "Information Age".

The environment in Indiana was particularly ripe for a co-ordinated response to the challenge of the electronic environment. For almost 20 years the State government had funded co-operative library networking through a programme called Area Library Service Authorities (ALSA). For the ten years prior to 1994, these networks had received no increase in public funding. The result was that the ALSAs were spending an increasingly large percentage of their funding on administration and record keeping. When the high overhead costs of the eight ALSAs became apparent, the Indiana Library and Historical Board forced a network consolidation resulting in a single library network (INCOLSA) serving almost all of the libraries (school, public, academic, and special) in the state. The network consolidation, which was understandably distressful for the library community in Indiana, had the compensatory benefit of forging highly co-operative relationships between various library constituencies, including the Indiana State Library, the Indiana Library Federation, and other library groups.

In 1995 and 1996, thanks to a substantial State budget surplus and new revenue from State-sponsored gambling, the state legislature was able to grant libraries $1m annually for technology innovation. The Indiana State Library, through INCOLSA, distributed this money for computer purchase, Internet connectivity and other computing-related technology innovation. The librarians of Indiana, led by INCOLSA, the Indiana State Library and the Indiana Library Federation, invited legislators, community leaders and others to a series of workshops to show what had been done with the technology money. These workshops entitled "Windows On the World" or "WOW", were well attended and much appreciated. Every attendee at each WOW workshop was invited to fill out an application for a Virtual Library Card. Following the WOW workshops, INCOLSA invited OCLC FirstSearch and NetFirst, Encyclopaedia Britannica, IAC's InfoTrac Searchbank and other non-commercial resources, such as Indiana and federal government resources, to participate in a demonstration. INCOLSA created a "glitzy" Web page with links to databases (http://www.palni.edu/~susan/inspire.html). Instead of simply listing the names of databases, the Web page listed subsets of databases under user-oriented headings such as:

Information for:

- Business and Professional Searchers

- Consumers & Community Resources

- Educators, Parents & Students

- General Information Explorers

- Government Agents & Clientele

The WOW workshops were well received and resulted in a legislative appropriation of $1m per year for database acquisition. Even before the legislative appropriation, the libraries of Indiana had begun working toward implementing a state-wide virtual library system. The INCOLSA Executive Director invited a group of librarians representing various library constituencies in Indiana to attend a planning meeting. The library groups that sent representatives to planning meetings included: Indiana Department of Education, Indiana State Library, Indiana Library Federation, Administrators of Large Public Libraries, the Private Academic Library Network of Indiana, and representatives from the public universities of Indiana and Indiana's small libraries. The INCOLSA Board of Directors authorised INCOLSA to act as the fiscal agent for INSPIRE and the librarian volunteers began functioning as the

INSPIRE Steering Committee. The Steering Committee later became the Advisory Committee of the Indiana State Library. To help with planning, the Steering Committee created a Technical Advisory Committee and a Database Selection Committee.

Ten database vendors responded to a set of specifications drawn up by the Database Selection Committee. Four vendor finalists in the selection process came to Indianapolis to demonstrate their products. From these, the offering from EBSCO was deemed most responsive to the INSPIRE proposal.

In addition to the $1m from the State legislature, INCOLSA received a grant of approximately $450,000 from Library Service and Technology Appropriation (LSTA) from the Indiana State Library. This money was used to install telecommunications, purchase a SUN server and firewall, and to employ a Project Manager and System Manager for INSPIRE.

Because INSPIRE was intended to go beyond serving databases to perform the additional functions of a virtual library, INCOLSA petitioned and received a grant from the Lily Foundation for $150,000 to purchase Z39.50 server software and to develop an expert search interface and a children's interface. After considering currently available alternatives, the SiteSearch/WebZ Z39.50 software from OCLC was selected.

INSPIRE respectfully acknowledges the Galileo system in Georgia as the pioneer model. Where INSPIRE goes beyond Galileo is that it serves a wider multi-type library community and it is the first state-wide system to serve end-users in their homes, offices, and school rooms as well as in libraries. A chief problem in serving end-users, wherever they can get on the Internet, is in user authentication. There are numerous possible solutions to this problem, but with 5.5m possible users, most solutions using name and password recognition are expensive. The initial solution to this problem is to use IP numbers and IP number ranges. Approximately 200 Internet Service Providers (ISPs) in Indiana can identify Indiana residents by their IP number. IP numbers cannot be used to identify Indiana resident clients of national ISP's such as AOL and CompuServe. The solution being pursued at this time is to employ digital certificates.

As the system neared completion we faced the problem of training. Would libraries, particularly small public and school libraries, be able to connect to the server? Once connected, how much training would be required to make the system useful? To answer these questions we selected ten libraries. We gave these libraries the URL of INSPIRE and asked them to try to connect to and use the system, only calling us when they reached the point where they needed help to continue. The questions were soon answered. Within 48 hours the URL had escaped into the Internet and the system was being used by dozens of libraries. There have been isolated problems and we have provided system and search interface training, but thus far the system has proven to be remarkably easy to install and use. We followed the opening of INSPIRE with training on advanced features of system administration and advanced searching techniques.

Current status

The first phase of INSPIRE (public access to online databases) became operational in January 1998. By June 1998, users of the system across the state of Indiana had access to the indexed data from approximately 4,500 journals, of which the contents of approximately 3,500 were available in full-text. The system was being used approximately 20,000 times each day and approximately 2m pages of full-text had been downloaded.

The databases available included:

- Academic Search Elite

- Business Source Elite

- Colliers Encyclopaedia

- Encyclopaedia of Animals

- ERIC

- Funk and Wagnall's New Encyclopaedia

- Health Source Plus

- Kid's Middle Grades Search +

- Kid's Primary Search

- MasterFILE FT 1500

- MAS FT Premier

- MEDLINE

- Newspaper Source

Criteria for success

To other states or groups wishing to implement a virtual networked library, we advise that four things are necessary:

Vision - someone needs to clearly enunciate an objective. There is no single "correct" vision and the vision may be modified by contribution from participants, but without a vision, significant achievement is unlikely. INSPIRE and Galileo can serve as a point of reference, but every time and every place must find its own mission.

Will to co-operate - in each community, individual libraries, different types of libraries, and different library organisations compete with each other for scarce resources - personnel and money. Only when these competing interests feel that there is more to gain by co-operating than by competing is the vision achievable.

Organisation - seldom is lack of resources, talent or will the limiting factor in realising co-operative programmes. The failure is usually due to the lack of a structure that will allow the effective deployment of resources.

Money - there is no substitute for money! But money alone is a poor substitute for vision, the will to co-operate, and an effective organisation. Of the four factors, we submit that money is the least difficult to obtain. Where there is a clear consensus, vision, a co-operative mentality and an effective organisation, it is relatively easy to attract sufficient funding.

Future developments

With the last components of the database portion of the virtual networked library being deployed, INSPIRE is looking forward to other subsystems. Our guide is this: any service that a user can obtain from a library by going into a library building should be a candidate for the service to be provided electronically to that person's computer terminal. We anticipate that new information services not currently possible will reveal themselves as we proceed with the evolution of the virtual networked library. Currently, however, there are some obvious candidates for inclusion in the virtual networked library:

Databases - our initial suite of databases is representative but not comprehensive. Our first priority is to add databases to complement those currently available on INSPIRE.

Library-quality Internet resources - historically, libraries have played a role as a quality filter of information. Libraries are the memory of human civilisation. We trust our history, in part, because libraries have collected the best and discarded the rubbish. There is no comparable filter on the Internet. The highest quality peer reviewed information has equal prominence with advertising, self-promotion, and pornography. Libraries **could** perform their valuable historical function if they were to authenticate and serve a library-quality subset of the information available on the Internet. We are considering using OCLC's NetFirst or an equivalent subset, or collecting our own subset.

Interlibrary loan of journals - a significant portion of our online databases is in full-text, but much of that database is available only in index format. We are considering installing an Indiana union list of serials with an interlibrary loan feature that would allow end-users to make interlibrary loan requests from their terminal.

Interlibrary loan of books - we are considering mounting a union list of all of the books held by all of the libraries in Indiana with an end-user initiated interlibrary loan capability.

Virtual reference service - some libraries and library networks allow users to ask reference questions by email. We are considering a networked library reference service. Users would be able to ask reference questions from their terminals. The question would go to the user's library. If the library could not answer that question for any reason (lack of reference materials, reference librarian busy, or library closed) the question would be forwarded to a reference centre. This service would allow specialisation of reference service and might allow libraries to provide equal or better reference service with fewer total reference staff.

We are not certain which of these or some other service will be our next step into the world of the virtual networked library. But we have seen that funding is not the greatest problem. When we have identified what we want to do, and we have gained consensus that the goal we select will provide the greatest benefit to our clients, we can raise the money and we can achieve our objectives in a remarkably short time.

References

1. Benton Foundation. *Buildings, books and bytes: Libraries in the Digital Age.* 1996. (copies can be requested from the Benton Foundation, 1634 I St., NW, 12th Floor, Washington, DC. USA.)

Spokes in the wheel:
links in the Sunderland Telematics Strategy

Conn Crawford

Senior Policy Officer (Information Society)
City of Sunderland

Abstract

The City of Sunderland Partnership's *"Telematics Strategy"* was first published in 1996. The paper examines its framework, mission, and core themes of infrastructure, inward investment, lifelong learning and quality of life. A range of different projects under its three main work areas of education and training; business; and the intelligent citizen, are described.

The impact of telematics - on citizens, on communities, on workers, on consumers, on education and on business – is considered. Librarians are recognised as having a huge contribution to make and urged to come to the centre stage in order to promote community-based lifelong learning.

The Telematics Strategy

The City of Sunderland Partnership's *"Telematics Strategy"*[1] was launched in 1996 at the University of Sunderland. It was the result of a distinctive collaboration between key agencies in Sunderland. So much has been achieved in the last two years that the strategy is already under review. Over 70 partners are involved at present in the re-draft of the policy with a view to completing it by Spring 1999.

The Telematics Strategy is developed and implemented by two sub-groups, COSIT (City of Sunderland Informatics/Telematics Forum) and COSTIG (City of Sunderland Telematics Implementation Group). The strategy has earned widespread recognition for the call centres at Doxford Park Business Centre and the Teleport.

The mission is:

> *"To raise awareness and skill levels of individuals and organisations within the City of Sunderland in the broad areas of IT and Telematics and by doing so enhance quality of life, increase business activity, maximise inward investment and ensure that Sunderland achieves and maintains a premier position in a knowledge-based future."*

Core themes

The Strategy is written around a number of core themes:

- infrastructure

- inward investment

- lifelong learning

- quality of life

From these come the three main work areas described below. These strands spawn a range of projects, ranging from initiatives to encourage community participation and feedback through the development of access points, to making computers more available through recycling schemes, setting up electronic village halls and developing the infrastructure in the Wheel of Opportunity, of which more later.

Intelligent City: including projects on intelligent democracy; intelligent housing estate; computer recycling; wheel of opportunity; electronic village halls;

unemployed and IT project; cyberskills; beyond cyberskills; Web factory; library integration and access; cybercafe; IT exhibition; and establishing the Sunderland Host.

Education and Training: projects include schools and colleges awareness; upstream call centre training; European language courses; Lifelong Learning online pilot.

Business: projects include the Teleport at Doxford International Business Park; Wear IT; Telebus awareness and promotion; Telematic Business start-up facilities; the networking and IT support centre; Make IT Grow; teleworking pilot.

Electronic village halls

Electronic village halls are community-based centres which provide IT facilities in areas of low employment. The first electronic village hall was launched in February 1998, at Pennywell Community Business. In the first six months:

- over 120 members of the estate have received training

- 12 businesses have benefited from, for example, sub-contract information

- new larger premises have been opened

- around 50 people have joined "Fat ladies on the Web"

- over 30 people have moved on to accredited IT courses

Although the Strategy only aimed to establish three electronic village halls, eight have been required during the first six months, due to demand.

Cyberskills

- already over 2,500 people have had access to telematics training through the University of Sunderland

- content has been extensively revised

- the project is self-sustaining after original pump-priming

Library integration and access

- LASH – the Libraries Access Sunderland Scheme has been established. This is being covered by Andrew McDonald in a separate session

- a city-wide licence has been bought to give access to over 2,000 electronic publications via EbscoHost

- we are working towards a single Web catalogue by the year 2000. A lot of work is needed in moving and integrating systems to make this possible

- the Public Libraries Challenge Fund for a regional libraries network will make it possible to link Sunderland libraries with others in the region

Establishment of the Sunderland Host

This is the City's Internet service established at the University of Sunderland to offer a commercial service to the community, so that we do not rely on external commercial services. This is a strategic necessity to preserve our independence. It allows us to develop content and to build in flexibility more easily. More than that, it is seen as the City Gateway and will go from strength to strength. Around 140 National Grid for Learning schools will link via the Host by the end of 1998.

Schools and colleges

All schools and 21 public libraries will be connected to the National Grid for Learning by the end of 1998, a crucial part of the Wheel of Opportunity.

Upstream call centre training

- over 4,500 jobs have been created in the last two and a half years, with another 2000 to come

- 200 unemployed people have been trained in the first year

- 300 will be trained each year up to the year 2000

- pre-training tasters will be arranged via Electronic Village Halls

Establish Teleport

The Teleport gives computer access to communications world-wide forming a gateway for the City and the region. We recognise the importance of establishing partnerships to develop content and to make the best use of the Teleport. Key milestones are:

- a consortium was established in March 1998

- satellite earth station will be installed by July 1998

- new technology is established locally, for example the Internet Voice Node is the first in the region

Telematic business start-up facilities

Over 40 companies have already been housed, and over 200 jobs created.

The Wheel of Opportunity

The aim is to establish a network throughout the City, linking the University, the City Council, sports centre, households, Cable TV operators, schools and the Careers Service, the City of Sunderland College and training providers, the Training and Enterprise Council, job centres and libraries, the Regional Technology Centre, Doxford International Teleport, Construction Industry Training Boards, 100 SMEs, the voluntary sector, major employers, and the Chamber of Commerce. At first, it was planned to establish the network through cable companies, but technology is advancing so quickly that this may not be needed. In order to do something now, the City Council's telephone network and ISDN connection is being used.

Impact of Telematics

Telematics has had a tremendous impact. The following points serve to emphasise the tremendous achievements which can be delivered through successful collaboration, to ordinary people in all aspects of their lives.

On citizens:

- ability to participate more fully in local affairs

- better awareness of entitlement

- improved communications with the local authority

- easy access to public information

- enhanced library and information services

On communities:

- enhanced communications within and between community groups

- access to community based training

On workers:

- new employment opportunities

- flexible access to computer-based learning

- opportunities to work from home and from community centres

On consumers:

- online tourist information

- home banking

- home shopping

On education:

- distance learning
- access to online and multimedia resources
- work-based training – learning opportunities in the workplace
- collaborative research to tackle problems and develop ideas

On business:

- EDI to speed up business transactions and reduce costs

- video-conferencing to save time and money

- access to collaborative networks

- access to market information

- opportunities to exploit new markets

- better access to continental Europe

It is surprising how little the Strategy encompasses the full range of impacts. We now realise that health, for example, services to the elderly, is not covered. We need to think about services to the citizen and how everybody will be affected. There is some pressure to set priorities, but also a need to take a broad approach in developing content.

Anticipated outputs

Anticipated outputs over the three-year period up to the Year 2000 were calculated some years ago, although they did not include anything about services. They were as follows:

- 15,000 members of the community given access to Telematics who would otherwise not have had such access

- 33,000 additional people trained to at least basic level in telematics skills

- 1,000 additional people trained in advances level telematics and retained in City

- 200 new telematics-related business start-ups

- 1,750 new jobs created

- 2,000 jobs protected

Learning services – what can libraries offer?

There has been much talk about accessibility. In Sunderland there are 29 libraries, and 290,000 people. We need more centres! We need to encourage schools and voluntary organisations to offer centres. Libraries can enable others to function more effectively; they are trusted and respectable; but they need to come forward more to the centre of the Strategy.

I am not asking library workers to become community development workers (although they often are). The information management skills that library services can offer the Strategy need to be developed at the core.

The Sunderland Host has a lot to offer the city in terms of making it easier to access information. Technical competence needs to be married to information management skills in the city, and that is where library services have an important role to play.

References

1. City of Sunderland Partnership. *Telematics Strategy*. Sunderland: City of Sunderland Partnership. 1996.

The Norfolk and Norwich Millennium Library

Hilary Hammond

Acting Director of Cultural Services
Norfolk County Council

Abstract

The paper describes the work which is currently underway to create a new library in Norfolk, examining the likely demands on the new library, including a review of information gained from a user survey. It outlines plans for the library's facilities, including study spaces, electronic resources, electronic management systems, and professional support. The roles which will need to be filled by the staff of the new library are considered, as are the other uses for the building, including a business and learning centre, lecture theatre, tourist information centre and catering. The paper concludes with a brief outline of the way in which the project is being funded.

Acknowledgement

This landmark project is supported by the Millennium Commission with a grant of £30m. Out of about 14 national projects, it is the only one which involves a library. Local funding is from Norfolk County Council, Norwich City Council and commerce. The partnership and the project started when a fire destroyed the old premises. A number of questions had to be asked after the fire. Do we need a central library? How can technology help? What about the books?

Do we need a central library?

There are currently two sites about a mile and a half away from each other. We had to look at whether there was need to replace these libraries. Factors examined included increased flexibility in employment, the number of careers expected within a working lifetime, the contract culture, and globalisation of work.

How can technology help?

Do we still need books, desks and people? What part can digitisation play? In 1995, we anticipated that we needed a business plan that would enable a roll-over of desktop equipment every three years. Now, within three years, eighteen months is a normal time-span. This has become a serious worry for funding any aspect of library development.

We also had to look at content. Desktop computers are wonderful things, but is the content of quality? I was fascinated by the Library and Information Commission's stress on content and training, which is fundamental to everything we do. Content is crucial.

Internet access is currently available to about 4% to 10% of the UK population. We forecast that it would be about 15% to 23% in the next three years. The BBC's *'Computers Don't Bite'*[1] said it would be around 50% by the turn of the century, but I think this is a considerable overestimate. The USA is currently 33%, and demand seems to have plateaued. It is worth bearing in mind that in this country, 10% of homes still do not have a voice telephone. This nirvana of wonderful computer access is still likely to be restricted to the information-rich, and unavailable to most people.

What will happen to print publishing with the development of electronic media? We did some work in checking how things had changed over the last 35 years, and found that there had been a 300% increase in published monographs (the proportion of science titles was decreasing and humanities increasing). We forecast quite a considerable transfer to electronic data in some areas. This is significant because when you are planning a library you need to know how much space you will need. Incidentally, ours will be a very long-lived library. It is dedicated to the Millennium Commission Project for 125 years as part of the contract, although it will look quite different by then.

What about the books?

I do expect books will continue to be in use in some areas because they are simply the most convenient form. I would expect transfer to electronic data for:

- science

- technology

- business

- research papers

- citizen information

I would expect long-term use of books for:

- fiction

- poetry

- travel

- biography

- hobbies

- children

There may also be creative writing in electronic form, but it will undoubtedly continue in print.

The Millennium Library

We can expect a greater number of users from all age groups, including students and those undertaking lifelong learning opportunities and recreation, because of the pressures and changes in society. We will also need more professionally-qualified staff to solve increasingly complex enquiries from increasingly complex sources. I do not know whether they will be librarians but I have a strong feeling that librarians and adult education workers may merge as a profession to help people learn.

There will be greater pressure on study facilities, and we can expect to have to provide more study spaces with information and communications technology. This can cause huge financial problems. It will be some time before we can choose to spend acquisitions funds on either print or electronic sources; in the meantime we have to do both.

Hitchcock and Carr[2] forecast a rise from 1,300 electronic journals in October 1997 to 3,200 in 1998/99. This is another massive step in the range of electronic publishing. But the cheapest and most limited form of site licence for universities is at least 10% more than a paper subscription. This is a serious problem.

The other big issue is the jumps in ICT. In 1995, when we started the research for the Millennium Commission we had to do research into set-top boxes. I remember one Sunday morning in Norwich using the Web for the first time and finding research papers on forecasts for the development of set-top boxes for Web access from home. Three years ago, that was a highly experimental process. Today, using the Web is normal. We do not know what the next "jump" will be.

The user research we did in 1994 after the fire, through a telephone survey of 320 users of the previous Central Library, showed the following:

- 46% used the old library for study and leisure

- 31% used quick reference on more than half their visits

- 70% used study tables, and 74% of these used them for at least one hour per visit

- 45% made use of Geac 9000 terminals to find out about stock

- 71% had asked staff about stock

- 6% had tried and failed to use the Geac terminals

- 68% of those not currently using the terminals would find them useful in future

- 80% would use computer accessed reference material

- 41% said they would use IT information sources more frequently than existing reference material

We were trying to judge what the users wanted. In the old building, the choice was either enquiries or borrowing, it was almost as simple as that. These were expectations – the reality may be different.

The actual building will occupy around 4,500m^2 and will have the following features:

- seven subject departments

- a "branch" library

- 120,000 items on open shelves

- 150,000 items in reserve

- the 2nd Air Division Memorial Library, Norfolk Studies, and Record Office Secondary Search Room.

The Millennium Commission required us to work out what the minimum statutory library would be. It was decided, with the then Department of National Heritage, what that would be, and everything above that figure qualified for matching funding.

The branch library in the building will be open whenever the building is open. We expect it, in due course, to open 24 hours, using self-services.

Our plans include:

- 220 study desks, 59 with PCs, all with network capability

- major CD ROM (or later technology) databases, costed at 250 platters running concurrently

- new county-wide housekeeping system, including self-services and smart cards from DS Ltd

- electronic guiding system of historical newspapers and illustrations

- image database with museums, Record Office and the University of East Anglia

- more professionally-qualified staff (probably fewer staff dealing with routine functions, and a change in role for support staff to provide a greater social support for individual library users)

- greater understanding of information sources, and specifically IT-based sources

- greater understanding of the needs of our community

- greater productivity

We will need to fill roles such as:

- information seekers and mediators

- information publishers

- friends of individuals

- guides to literature, history and culture generally

- support to those who cannot reach our buildings

Other elements included in the building will be:

- heritage attraction

- business and learning centre

- Tourist Information Centre and ticket shop

- multi-media lecture theatre

- catering

- car park

- internal and external square

Costs:

- millennium building construction, fittings and fees will be £43.6m

- library service revenue growth

    - £661,000 for the Millennium Library

    - £85,000 for a new library housekeeping system

The County Council has agreed this major growth in revenue expenditure, without which we could not have submitted the bid.

References

1. Computers Don't Bite" (15/6/98). BBC Television.

2. Hitchcock, S., Carr, L., Hall, W., 1997. "Web journals publishing: a UK perspective" Serials, Nov. Also at http://journals.ecs.soton.ac.uk/uksg.htm

Networked learning through the libraries of Europe: from vision to reality

Ian Pigott

Principal Administrator
European Commission, DG XIII

Abstract

After a brief overview of how the Commission's involvement in applied Research and Development in the library sector has contributed to a general improvement in the IT-related skills of library staff, the paper describes progress on a number of projects addressing distance learning. Consideration is then given to how current and future national and European programmes accommodate libraries and education, particularly in relation to lifelong learning.

Introduction

It was in the late 1980s that the European Commission started to prepare the ground in order to support networked library services across Europe. These early developments soon led to projects under the first Telematics Programme (1991-1993) which in turn led to a more consolidated approach in the current Telematics Applications Programme (1994-1998).

As a result, we have now embarked on some 100 collaborative projects and support actions, many of which have already been completed. These, in conjunction with studies, workshops and concertation activities, have done much to keep libraries informed of the opportunities open to them in the emerging information society. Above all, they have acted as a catalyst in encouraging librarians to become directly involved in transnational networks and related skills.

It is, therefore, heartening to see that today libraries across Europe not only provide a number of sophisticated resource and information services based on Internet access but that national authorities are also beginning to recognise their importance as participants in the area of lifelong learning.

Our two work programmes

Our initial programme, which began in 1991, was designed to build up momentum and generate hands-on experience. It set out to start a process of change in order to modernise libraries and their services. The current work plan (1994-1998) takes the process one step further forward by integrating and expanding the results already achieved in order to bring about a truly European-wide approach to networked library services.

For those who like statistics, we have

- 51 co-funded projects under the first programme and 32 under the second

- three support actions under the first programme and 14 under the second

- 28 background studies

- 14 workshops and conferences

Typical components of European projects

Before we look a little more closely at projects in the area of distance learning, it may be useful for you to have details of how projects are set up and funded.

Projects are selected through calls for proposals evaluated by outside experts. Partners must be located in at least two different countries (usually four or more) and must always include at least one library. Other partners may consist of networking specialists, software houses, publishers, research departments or universities. They are often joined by a number of associate partners, often libraries, who also play a key role in the validation and demonstration phases.

European shared-cost co-operative projects have for the most part been modest in their scope and funding, particularly when compared to initiatives in the United States. For example, with a couple of exceptions, the 51 projects under the initial programme had overall budgets of some £500,000, about half of which was normally covered by programme funding. The projects in the current programme are slightly larger in scope, total budgets averaging around £800,000. In the initial programme, as in the current one, project duration typically varies between about 18 months and three years.

Project deliverables include reports, many of which are directly accessible via the Web. Indeed, as in eLib, nearly all our projects have their own Web sites, providing a rapid and convenient means of distributing information to partners across Europe, while promoting project developments for the world at large. In the current programme, there is strong emphasis on new services (in contrast to technical innovation), encouraged by the demonstration, validation and dissemination phases which form part of each and every project. This emphasis, intended to ensure that user needs and reactions are taken fully into account, is designed to promote technology take-up and shorten the gap between R&D developments and the market place.

The areas covered

The main objectives of our earlier work were to improve accessibility to modern library services in Europe, to catalyse the take-up of new technologies in libraries and to provide for both technical standardisation and harmonisation of national policies in regard to library networking. The resulting areas of action specifically covered bibliographic resources, library interconnections, library services and the development of new products for libraries.

The current programme (1994-1998) is even more clearly focused on the move in the libraries world from collection-based services to those dealing with electronic access. It provides support for internal library developments toward the networked world, for interconnected library services drawing on a distributed library resource in Europe and for access to global electronic information assets by means of resource discovery technologies and library-mediated services. In this respect, the focus of most of our projects may, therefore, seem rather broader than under eLib.

Our projects have to date involved over 430 participants. Partnerships have consisted principally of libraries of various types (60%), and SMEs, research institutes and universities (30%).

Encouraging progress is now being made in the areas of networking technology and a wide range of services including, for example, children's library services, music, access to electronic journals, service models for distributed services, single-card access to resources and Web support for public libraries. Details of projects and other activities can be accessed via our Web site at http://www.echo.lu/libs/ .

Distance learning projects

While all our projects have to some extent contributed to the distance learning scene, in that they have promoted the step-by-step development of networked library services, we have supported a number of initiatives which have directly addressed the problem of supporting education and training through libraries. Projects initiated under the first programme included:

BIBDEL   Libraries without walls: the delivery of library services to distant users. A toolkit of techniques was developed as a practical and cost-effective guide to learners throughout Europe.

EDUCATE   End-user courses in information access through communication technology. Courseware in electrical engineering and physics was the starting point for a successful series of modules in a variety of subjects. Attention is also given to the training of librarians in the distance learning environment.

HYPERLIB   Hypertext interfaces to library information systems. One of our first projects to recognise the importance of the Web in providing remote access to libraries.

MURIEL   Multimedia education system for librarians introducing remote interactive processing of electronic documents. Provided support for education and training for librarianship in the networked environment.

PLAIL   Public libraries and adult learners. Paved the way for access to distance learning through public libraries and contributed to librarian training.

All these helped to build awareness of the problems to be solved but it has been mainly under our current programme that we have really started to make a contribution to the needs of distance learners of all types.

ELVIL   The European legislative virtual library. This project is developing Web-based resources and references on European law and politics including an educational aid for students, teachers and librarians.

CHILIAS   Children in libraries: improving multimedia virtual library access and information skills. Of interest here as a result of the importance given to training children to make good use of Web-based resources.

VERITY   Virtual and electronic sources for information skills training. A new project aimed at guiding teenagers in finding and managing information held in libraries and on electronic networks.

DERAL   Distance education in rural areas via libraries. Will assist public library involvement in distance learning services, especially for those living in rural areas.

DEDICATE   Distance education information courses through networks. Built on the EDUCATE approach, will develop distance education courses in information literacy for academic libraries in five Eastern-European countries.

LIBERATOR   Libraries in European regions - access to telematics and other resources. Provides access to a wide variety of information resources to large regional public library networks.

National policies

It is encouraging to see how many specific national developments are now taking place across Europe on networked library services. In addition to the eLib and EARL initiatives in the UK and all the developments in connection with the New Library programme, there is considerable activity in all the Nordic countries, which now specifically include libraries as an important component of their planning for the information society.

France, with its recent Information Society Action Plan, addresses libraries in connection with cultural heritage and multimedia services.

Portugal's *Saber Disponível* (accessible knowledge) panel proposes to make networked information accessible through public libraries. In Spain there are proposals to set up *telebibliotecas* (networked libraries) to enable users to access local, regional, national and international networked information.

Indeed, most EU Member States are now developing plans for active participation in the information society and, increasingly, importance is given to libraries, particularly in connection with education and training.

The Green Paper and library participation in the Information Society

Many of you will be aware that last year the European Parliament called on the Commission to prepare a green paper on the role of libraries in the information society. We began this work by compiling extensive background information on how the library scene is developing in the Member States and, in addition, we have paid particular attention to matters such as cultural identity, lifelong learning, copyright, literacy and cost of services, not forgetting the key issue of how libraries can best help to close the gap between the information rich and the information poor in the years ahead.

Recently, the European Parliament's Committee on Culture, Youth, Education and the Media decided to prepare a so-called "own initiative report" on the role of libraries. As a result, we have had a number of contacts with the rapporteur, Mrs Ryynänen who has responded by drawing on our background material and findings. Her report is now circulating in draft form for amendments.

In the context of education, it is interesting to note that the report emphasises the significance of knowledge (the most important resource of the information society), and of access to it, and explains how important it is for citizens to be able to use libraries in order to satisfy their individual needs for information.

It is expected that the report will be debated at the European Parliament in July or September, calling on the Commission and the Member States to address a number of issues in its R&D activities and elsewhere.

The future

Next year will also see the start of the EU's Fifth Framework Programme for Research and Development which will provide specific support for "Creating a User-Friendly Information Society". We are now progressing rapidly on the work programme for the key actions. One of the goals - under Key Action 3 - is to develop widely-accessible services based on multimedia content. Libraries, with other public institutions such as museums, galleries and archives, will have a new role to play, namely that of strengthening the emerging knowledge and culture economy by providing mediated access to these rapidly evolving resources.

Given the firm emphasis on new services in the current round of projects, libraries and their partners should be able to move forward smoothly into new levels of involvement. The integration of print and digital information will ultimately allow users to benefit from a whole range of seamlessly-integrated services. Not only will there be a long-term goal of ensuring continuity of access for future generations but, over the next few years, new business and economic models will also be required for managing access to vastly expanded and widely distributed stores of digital information.

Today's conference is timely. The UK has clearly recognised the challenges and opportunities for libraries in the learning community. It is particularly fitting that the conference should be held here, in the North East, which is contributing so actively to projects in the library sector based on European partnerships.

Ten years ago, many of the topics addressed at this conference were mere dreams. Today some of them have become reality. But we must now move forward to the new opportunities unveiled by the Internet and the global information society. Consolidation of the roles of both academic and public libraries in providing access to knowledge and learning for all the citizens of Europe is not just a vision but a technically achievable goal.

Singapore: the intelligent island

Professor Nick Moore

Senior Partner
Acumen UK

Abstract

The paper briefly describes Singapore in geographical, political and socio-economic terms, then looks at the specific economic situation which has led to major development in Singapore to create the "intelligent island".

Three phases of development are described: computerisation, networking, and application and content. The resulting network, Singapore ONE, has a wide range of applications, including education programmes, information, entertainment, business and government functions. There is a strong emphasis throughout on learning, both learning to use the applications, and also in creating a learning society.

The system is seen by everyone involved in its development as part of a wide industrial, social, economic, cultural and political process which is part of a seamless whole.

Background

For those who do not know it, Singapore is about the size of the Isle of Wight, and lies in relation to the Malaysian mainland in much the same way as the Isle of Wight does to the British mainland. It is very small geographically, and is dominated by Malaysia to the north, on which it is wholly dependent for its water supply, and by Indonesia to the south about twenty miles away. Both countries have different population mixes, religious structures and different sorts of political structure, and so Singapore feels itself to be in a fairly vulnerable position, and this is worth remembering in terms of their plans for the future.

There is a small population of about 2.5m which is so densely packed that it cannot expand beyond 3m in terms of economic growth, unlike some countries in the area.

There is also a very strong Confucian ethos, and this is important. The sense of community and sense of communitarian spirit within the country runs very strong. As an individual, one's loyalty is first to the family, then to the community and then to the state, very definitely in that order, and last to yourself. The idea of individual responsibility, individual freedom and so on is very much constrained and managed by one's role within the family and within the community and the state. That is important in understanding many of the criticisms that are levelled at Singapore.

Economic situation

They have had over 20 years of rapid economic growth, at rates of around 7% to 9% a year (not consistently - it dipped in the 1980s) and that is the norm they expect. For those of us who have lived in Britain for the last 20 years with a growth rate fluctuating between 1.5% and 2% on good years, Singapore is a very exciting place to live. The sense of growth and expectation about how things are going to be bigger and better next year runs through a whole generation and conditions very much the way people think in that part of the world.

They decided to create Singapore as the "intelligent island", as the hub or the centre in that part of the world where multinational companies could base their regional headquarters. It is designed to be the place within the region which is the centre for high-tech in medicine, for very high-quality education, for cultural development, and so on. They wanted to position themselves as the regional centre for that whole dramatically expanding, fairly volatile area. To do that they have gone through three phases of development:

- from 1985 until about 1990 they concentrated on computerisation, implementing computers and automated processes

- from 1990-1995 they concentrated on networks, and building Singapore as a "wired island"

- from 1995 until the present they have focused on applications and content

Computerisation 1985-1990

This was the direct response to the new economic policy document prepared in 1985. There was an economic downturn around that time, and growth rates dropped to about 5% from 8%, causing a lot of concern. A new economic committee was formed to produce a new economic policy, and it gave a very clear analysis. They needed an economic goal to work towards. The goal they set themselves was to have, by the end of the century, a standard of living equivalent to whatever the standard of living was at that time for the people of Switzerland. This represented a massive growth in the economy and standard of living. The only way to manage, given the domination to the north and south, and the constraints on size and population, was to add more value per worker. It was decided that there must be a move out of heavy industry and engineering, where they had built their success over the last 15 years, and move into high value-added processes. This was done in a number of stages, starting with a move into assembling of electronics, then into design of electronic goods, with regional centres for the manufacture of the designs, delivery, marketing and so on.

In order to obtain more value per worker it was necessary to become more familiar with using IT, to create a demand and market for IT in Singapore. Through computerisation, Government estimated the supply of programmers and so on. So the National Computer Board was created, and given the remit to computerise Government in two and a half years. This was achieved! In the process they have trained an enormous number of people, delivered a very new approach towards the analysis of system requirements, and learnt on a very steep learning curve how to computerise and make good use of computers.

Networking 1990-1995

This left them in a good position for the next step. Five years later they needed to link everything together: the focus was on building the networks. There was another economic policy document in 1990 and a plan to take them into the next century, adding more value per worker, moving up the value chain, moving up the technology ladder and becoming smarter. The National Computer Board's response was *"IT 2000: the vision of an intelligent island"* in which they not only made very intensive use of computers and IT but they also linked them all together and built them into networks, and started using them for many more dynamic purposes. In order to do that they created a broadband network, which is not so difficult to do in a very compact country and this network links businesses, blocks of flats and government offices. This was achieved over a five year period, mostly with public investment, but with some private enterprise investment as well.

Applications and content 1995 to the present

By about 1995, they had the expertise, and networks and they then needed applications and content to spin around the network.

Singapore ONE is one network for everyone. It consists of the network connecting and linking up individual businesses and homes to the ATM network using ASDL.

Also, logically, they have a whole set of applications. Over the period from about 1996, a lot of effort has gone into encouraging application providers, the public sector, the education sector and also the private sector to develop applications. These were piloted until the beginning of June 1998, and from 1 June 1998, a full service was in operation. People pay for it. During the pilot there were 40,000 homes linked up to it: they are aiming for 100,000 by the end of this year and, eventually, for half a million. Effectively everybody will be linked.

There is now a high capacity service. The network delivers into people's homes flows of information that are 100 times faster than a 28.8 kilobit modem. The delivery of 3D graphics, video, CD-quality sound, and much more, has now been discussed. A wide range of applications has been developed by the public sector, who took the lead. Each government department and agency was expected to develop applications which could be delivered over this network: the educational institutions have huge distance learning programmes on it; the tax office has all its information on it; you can interact with government wholly in electronic mode. There are also a large number of private sector suppliers. The material falls into five strands:

- information

- entertainment

- business to business

- education

- government

There is a very strong emphasis throughout on learning, not only learning how to use each other's different applications but also on creating a learning society. The rhetoric of having to create a learning society in order to take advantage of the information society runs very strongly.

There are a number of important characteristics and lessons we can learn. The system is fully integrated into the national economic development policy. It is not an add-on or a desirable extra, but part of a much wider industrial, social, economic, cultural and political development process. It is part of a seamless whole, and is seen like that by everyone involved in its development.

The VALNOW service:
reaching the distant learner

Professor Peter Brophy

Director of the Centre for Research in Library & Information Management
Manchester Metropolitan University

Abstract

VALNOW – the Virtual Academic Library of the North West – is an operational service which delivers library services to a widely-dispersed student population across North West England. In this paper, the origins of VALNOW are described, starting with the identification of remote users' needs through university quality assurance processes and through a national project on students' actual experiences of library services, to an international development project funded by the European Commission. The establishment of VALNOW as a service, and the development options which now present themselves, are then described.

Introduction

I should first of all make clear that, although when I was asked to make this presentation I was the Head of the University of Central Lancashire's Library and Learning Resource Services, with direct responsibility for the VALNOW service, I have since moved to Manchester Metropolitan University, where I continue to direct the Centre for Research in Library and Information Management, but have no remaining responsibility for VALNOW. My comments today, therefore, must be taken to apply to the development of the service and its initial operation, and nothing I say can be construed to apply necessarily to the service as it now operates.

VALNOW stands for the *Virtual Academic Library of the North West*, so-called because it serves a widely-dispersed user population, from Liverpool in the South to Penrith in the North, and includes widely different locations, from industrial conurbations to some of the remotest rural areas to be found in England. Many, probably most, of the users have probably never visited the University Library in Preston which is at the hub of the service. This is not surprising, as they could be based 100 km or more from that campus.

The users are "franchise course" students, clustered in groups at further education or similar college sites, but undertaking university courses under franchise arrangements – meaning that the University retains control of quality assurance and awards, but delivery of the course is in the hands of college staff. The typical student would have entered higher education via an access course, or perhaps with NVQs rather than the traditional school/'A' level route, and many are mature, perhaps with family responsibilities. Without support on this or some other model, they would almost certainly have been excluded from higher education. It is also worth noting that many of the areas served were suffering in economic terms from the lack of a university presence, with its ability to deliver highly-trained staff and to act as a driver for economic activity and technological development. Indeed, Cumbria is one of the few counties in England with no university and certainly one of the largest areas to be so deprived. It should also be noted that Cumbria offers peculiar geographical challenges, since its most populous areas are spread around the perimeter of a mountainous region with very poor road and rail communications between them.

Origins of VALNOW

The origins of VALNOW can be traced back to three main strands. Two, based on particularly apt research and development programmes, will be dealt with in the next sections. The first, however, was a series of formal reports on the operation of franchised courses. As the Chair of one of the University's Review Panels (the bodies charged with overseeing quality assurance), I was aware that one of the main complaints of students was not that the teaching they experienced was in any way inferior to that available on campus, but simply that the resources, and in particular the library resources, did not compare. One of the axioms of franchise provision is that students should receive an equivalent – which is not to say identical – experience, whether they are on or off-campus. It was clear that in terms of library provision this was not the case. It was, even with the best intentions, impossible for colleges to create libraries on the scale and with the riches of a university library and no one was seriously suggesting that such libraries should be built in remote locations across the North West.

A limited number of actions were taken to try to deal with this situation. Some help could be offered by ensuring that the franchise course students could use the main University library if they visited in person, but given the distances this was clearly an inadequate response to their needs. A 'Partner Colleges Library Network' was set up to ensure that University and College library staffs were talking to one another, and that there was awareness of the library demands likely to be posed by different academic programmes. University library staff put forward a detailed analytical report to every franchise validation event, where a decision would be made whether or not to approve a proposal to run a course in a particular location. Helpful as these measures were, they were clearly not enough.

Researching the student experience

By 1991, it was clear that we needed to find new solutions to the problem of serving students who were distant from the University campus. However, before rushing into the design of services, we felt that it was important to gain a deeper understanding of the student experience. With funding from the British Library's then Research & Development Department, we undertook an 18 month, in-depth study of student use. This research has been reported elsewhere[1]. It involved detailed studies of both franchise course students and control groups based on campus. The methodologies used included interviews, focus groups and diary studies – this last one involved students in recording their information-seeking in specific situations tied to the completion of coursework assignments.

The title of a workshop held towards the end of the project neatly summed up the findings of this work, and was taken from the comment of one student on a franchised course: "There must be more". Students were using a wide variety of coping strategies to overcome the limitations of the facilities available locally. They would share books that they had bought, borrow from tutors, use the public library or, as more than one focus group admitted, simply make up answers to assignments by using their imaginations! But there were also positive aspects to being a franchise course student. Group bonding was a tremendous support, and they were never overwhelmed by the scale of the resources available as some of their on-campus counterparts were.

It should be emphasised that at this stage, 1992-93, the IT facilities available to these students were by today's standards quite primitive, even if they existed at all. There were very few relevant online services available, and most were priced on a per-usage basis which effectively excluded undergraduate use. The World Wide Web was something that few had heard of, and in any case was clearly going to be of little use outside the scientific research community for which it had been designed! Networks were slow, and although the Joint Academic Network (JANET) existed, it linked only major campuses and was of little relevance to off-campus delivery or to teaching.

Developing a new model of service delivery

In 1993 we put forward a proposal to the European Commission under the *Telematics for Libraries* Programme for a project called *BIBDEL: The Delivery of Library Services to Distant Users*. The proposal was selected for funding and in 1994 this major new project was launched. As with all projects in the Telematics Programme, BIBDEL was a co-operative project with cross-European involvement. The Centre for Research in Library & Information Management (CERLIM) had been established at the University of Central Lancashire in 1993, and was the co-ordinating partner. We were joined by Dublin City University in the Republic of Ireland, which had national responsibility for higher education distance learning, using a model very different from that of the UK's Open University. The third partner was the University of the Aegean in Greece, a university spread across four islands in the Aegean with the obvious problems that presented for the delivery of library services.

The BIBDEL Project[2] (again the results have been reported extensively elsewhere) attempted to use readily available information and communications technologies to test out the feasibility of delivering library services at a distance. Where possible proprietary software was used, so that, for example, the UK part of the project made extensive use of the *Remotely Possible* tool. The Irish experiment, attempting to serve individual users, often at their homes, tried to use students' own equipment rather than expensive, state-of-the-art PCs. The University of the Aegean accepted the limitations of its existing library software and examined the ways of linking multiple sites, using that software base, to include document delivery.

While the project had significant implications for all European academic libraries, and has attracted considerable interest across Europe, its practical significance for the franchise course students of the University of Central Lancashire in North West

England was considerable. Indeed it is worth stressing that BIBDEL was one research project which led to very practical and sustainable outcomes.

BIBDEL demonstrated that low technology solutions – especially where there was a managed mix of IT-based and traditional approaches – could provide significant benefits to the remote user. Thus, while it was essential that the user could examine bibliographic and holdings data at a distance, and make requests online, the delivery of much information could be handled offline quite satisfactorily. Further, students would often prefer that a document (book or journal) be sent by post rather than sent in electronic form.

While it is not possible in this paper to elaborate on the findings of BIBDEL, it is perhaps worth recording that the project did provide evidence that, far from remote students overwhelming the service with demand, it was very much the case that library staff had to promote the service in order to generate significant levels of use. While to some extent this is a matter of demand building up over time, it did seem to the project team that excessive demand by remote users was unlikely to be a serious problem.

The launch of the VALNOW service

Following the success of BIBDEL and the continued success of the Partner Colleges Library Network, a decision was taken in 1996 to place the experimental BIBDEL service on a permanent footing and to extend its scope to all of the University's partner colleges. The service was formally launched in March 1997 at a ceremony at the University in Preston, at which the online link to each of the colleges was demonstrated.

Although there were delays in achieving full networking and some aspects of the service were slow to take off, the VALNOW service was able to offer a portfolio of services to the franchised course students (and, incidentally, to the staff teaching them). These services included:

- access to centrally-mounted datasets on CD-ROM (for which additional licence fees were paid by the University, not by the Colleges)

- access to JISC dataservices (it should be noted that since franchise course students were registered university students we had been paying charges for their access to such services anyway)

- access to the University OPAC, coupled with an additional facility to enable remote users to order items which were 'in Library' (meaning that they were on the main library shelves and not on loan)

- support for subject enquiries by videoconference link so that a student who was, say, starting work on a dissertation could obtain specialist advice.

The service was set up to be managed through a joint VALNOW Management Group with membership from the University library staff <u>and</u> College library staff.

Possible future developments

Services such as VALNOW clearly fill a real need and, given the developments which have been seen in networked information delivery in the last few years, there are major development opportunities. The University of Central Lancashire is a partner in the eLib funded HyLiFe (Hybrid Library of the Future) project (CERLIM being joint co-ordinator) and has particular responsibility for researching the application of the hybrid library concept in the distributed environment. The concept of 'clumps' is clearly relevant to VALNOW. At present, the only library catalogue available is that of the University – why not include the college libraries, local public libraries and other resources as well? Directory services, including sophisticated authentication of users operating in multiple environments, are a possibility. It could be that VALNOW would provide a useful testbed for the use of multifunctional smartcards, again operating across sectors. Materials are currently delivered to college sites, but, should home delivery become an option? What about on-campus students, they should not be disadvantaged or denied access to such attractive services?

Conclusion

VALNOW represents one attempt to deliver, in a very practical way, services which non-traditional higher education students need if they are to be enabled to make the most of their educational opportunities. It represents a serious attempt to provide a model for the academic library operating in a distributed environment in order to serve the needs of students whose learning is increasingly "lifelong". As such it is my hope that it will continue to develop and prosper.

References

1. Goodall, D. and Brophy, P. *A Comparable Experience? Library Support for Franchised Courses in Higher Education* (British Library Research & Innovation Report: 33) Preston: CERLIM, University of Central Lancashire, 1997.

2. Brinkley, M., Brophy, P., Butters, G., MacDougall, A., Papachiou, P. and Vlachou, E. *Access to Campus Library and Information Services by Distant Users: Final Report.* Preston: University of Central Lancashire, 1996.

The Utrecht Library:
partner in national and local experiments

Ineke Herweijer

Councillor
City of Utrecht, Netherlands

Abstract

After a brief outline of Utrecht and its population, the paper looks at the characteristics of a learning community and the ways in which Utrecht is developing in these areas. Partnerships have been established with schools for the last 20 years, and this has now been extended to playgroups and kindergartens, and will soon also include professional colleges. Collaboration is taking place in IT and other educational areas. There is also cooperation with the local university and the polytechnic.

The library is also involved in non-institutional partnerships, such as information skills training to help individual users to use the Internet and other electronic resources. The 'Moroccan Platform' is an initiative to help Moroccan groups in the same way.

The difficulties of the cost of access to electronic information and other difficulties are discussed, ending with some conclusions drawn from the Utrecht experience.

Introduction

I think it is important to tell you something about my city. You should know who lives there, how many inhabitants there are and where exactly Utrecht is!

Utrecht is the fourth biggest city of the Netherlands. We have only one big city, Amsterdam of course, but the main characteristics of a city are found in all four, and maybe even in more cities. Our history goes back to the beginning of our era: the Romans had a castellum at the border of their empire, the river Rhine, a small stream which still flows through the City and forms beautiful canals.

Utrecht has 235,000 inhabitants of which about 50,000 are immigrants. The number of immigrants is increasing (with a higher birth-rate than average). In primary schools, half of the population is from non-Dutch origin. 50% of them are Moroccan, 25% Turkish and there are at least 20 other nationalities.

The city can be characterised as a centre of knowledge, having the biggest university of the Netherlands (and one of the oldest, over six hundred years old!), a polytechnic and a professional college.

Commercial and non-profit services are important in Utrecht. It is the second financial centre of the Netherlands, after Amsterdam. Traditional industries have almost disappeared but modern high-tech enterprises are booming.

The city will experience many changes in the near future: new developments in housing (up to 20,000 new houses will be built before 2005. There is a new stop for the high-speed trains on the line to Germany and a huge reconstruction of the city centre near the railway station.

I have been Deputy Mayor of Utrecht for the last four years, charged with economic development (including tourism, employment and information technology), international co-operation, education and the libraries.

The theme of this conference is the role that libraries may play in the learning society, the changes and partnerships that are required.

In some sectors, we have many years experience and, in others, we are only at the beginning of developments which we hope will be facilitated by learning from best practice developed elsewhere.

Characteristics of the learning community

First of all, I want to speak about the characteristics of the learning community, of lifelong learning and about some trends in society. The amount of information that is available every day for our citizens is immense. In education the transfer of knowledge tends to be replaced, partially, by the teaching of how to learn. The capacity for acquiring information, studying and implementing it, is more and more important. These skills are essential not only within mainstream education or within employent, but also for recreational purposes, for hobbies and participation in society in general.

At the time when information and the need for it is growing, I see a certain tendency towards a more superficial approach. Zapping through the many channels on TV, looking at or studying short programmes with a dynamic but superficial content, the citizen is surfing through the information that is offered. There is too much information and it can only be taken in at a superficial level.

There is something else that should worry us. Many citizens do not automatically have access to all this information. Some lack the necessary skills and training but most lack the means to obtain access. The segregation between the have's and have-nots in the digital society is not new. The distance between them, however, is growing. Libraries are operating on the edge where information, education and training meet. The way in which this happens is changing but the role of libraries in society is still the same.

Gemeentebibliotheek Utrecht – Public Library

The municipal library of Utrecht is the oldest public library of the Netherlands and was founded in 1892. It has 165 employees in ten branches. The local Council wants the library to be the multicultural centre for information and knowledge for all our citizens.

Therefore the Library has three tasks:

- provision of a range of material for reference and borrowing

- the dissemination of information

- as a cultural centre and to provide information skills training

Around 50% of all primary school children are members of the library. They pay (until the age of 18) only five guilders a year and nothing at all if their family has a minimum wage. Adults pay a membership fee and a certain amount of money per book, CD, video etc. Around 20% of our adult population are members of the library.

As I said, we provide, books, magazines, videos, music, CD-ROM and electronic databases. In all branches, members can consult the Internet for free.

Partnerships with schools and colleges

For the last 20 years, the Library has been co-operating with schools. Special (national and local) funds for education to the less-privileged were partly used for this purpose.

Nowadays, this co-operation has been extended to playgroups and kindergarten. The activities consist of advice concerning the school's own libraries, training of teachers in using books and other material in their classes, class visits to the library, circulation of special collections (special items or circulating collections) and co-operation in projects. An annual subscription package is offered for schools and other institutions.

Quite promising are new initiatives for the creation of a so-called Digital Square for schools, the library, and other institutions, as well as the project "School library online" which brings services such as the catalogues into the school.

For two years, a similar service has been developed for secondary and professional schools. This co-operation is still growing. In secondary schools, the development of what we call a "study-house" (that is a system of individual learning with coaching by the teachers instead of more classical teaching) requires new methods of presenting information and knowledge.

Many teachers do not know yet how to be coaches rather than teachers and need professional training themselves. The library might play a role there. The main problem which we have to face, however, is the lack of budget for schools and libraries, in particular, for building a mediathèque or information centre which is sufficiently extensive to serve all students.

The 12 to 15 age group poses particular problems. Many students at this level have no reading background or any other skills in finding the information they need, unless they learn it at school. Therefore the library has offered inductions for 25 groups of students in the branch libraries.

The relationship with the professional colleges is at the very initial stages, as is the relationship with colleges for adults. An interesting proposal has been presented to the local Council recently: the Regional Centre for Professional and Adult Education and Training wants to build a new building for one of its sectors, therefore their learning facilities should be combined with one of the branches of the municipal library which also needs a new building in that neighbourhood. Thus the combination of information provided in the library and the learning facilities should lead to a more natural way of training for these professional students who, at the same time, might become more interested in what a modern library can offer them. This is a good example of co-operation with other institutions. The library also plays its role in more informal learning routines. I mentioned the high percentage of members who come to the library for their own study purposes. In the University libraries, students work until late at night in special rooms for individual study. I expect that this role will increase. The costs of information media are simply too high for the individual citizen.

Other partnerships

Utrecht's municipal library has long since had an additional task: apart from the usual collection, it maintains a so-called "top-collection" of a more scientific character for the whole region. One could ask why, since the University Library is nearby. This collection, however, is an addition to the University's collection, which is meant to be used by its own students, scientists and teachers. The purchases for this "top-collection" are selected in close collaboration with the University Library.

A modern initiative in this sector is the so-called Ruben project, which is to be completed by the end of 1998. The libraries of the University, the Polytechnic and the City have developed a virtual catalogue on the Internet, through which the catalogues of the three libraries may be consulted as one. The required item will then be delivered to the requestor's own library.

Non-institutional partnerships

A new task for our library is what we call media-education or information skills training. Since January 1997, the library has been running special sessions for those citizens who want to know more about the Internet and how to find their way in all the new media. The costs for the participants are minimal, especially for those on low wages, and so that large parts of the population take part, including many senior citizens!

Of course the library, as any other modern institution, wants to know the needs of its customers and extensive surveys are carried out regularly. As a result, we know there is a need for more extended opening hours. A new phenomenon is a council of experts in the fields of education, culture, mass-communication, information technology, broadcasting, publishing and so on. This council should advice the library about strategic questions and the library's role in the Utrecht community.

Moroccan parents

Since 1996, I have been the initiator of a Moroccan group, called "The Moroccan Platform", consisting of parents, teachers, students and community leaders, such as imams. They all want to improve the situation of their youngsters. One of their activities has been to bring more Moroccans to the library when special visits were organised. The Platform gives advice concerning the presentation of the library's material to Moroccan citizens of Utrecht, it organises group visits for children and parents, and it keeps an eye on any young ones who try to disturb the atmosphere in the library. The group was helpful in creating a special Internet course for adult Moroccans.

Two sessions have already taken place, and they were very successful.

The future

Since new media are being used in the libraries, new problems arise. The question of rights has not yet been solved, and I think this is a global problem. Our legislation has not yet been adapted for the dissemination of information via digital media that used to be paid for. Two things should be combined: the commercial rights of the authors of information and the free (or at least cheap and easy) access to information for all those who cannot afford it. Libraries cannot fulfil their task of bringing all the available knowledge and information to all our citizens if they have to pay huge sums to do so.

There is much more to say about the role of the library, especially in Utrecht. Think of entrepreneurs just starting or young professionals creating their own business. Their needs for information are not yet served by the library. Think of the changes that arise for the library staff who used to offer books, records or tapes and must now become consultants in the information market. Think of the role of national and local government who all too often base their funding of the libraries on the traditional tasks.

I will end with a few conclusions from our Utrecht experience:

- the library is the right place for informal learning

- participation in the local society starts with access to all those who need information

- the local community is the library's main partner

- we should find new ways of combining the commercial rights of authors and publishers with access to information and education for all our citizens.

Library partnerships for lifelong learning

Professor Robert Burgess

Pro Vice-Chancellor and Director of CEDAR
University of Warwick

Abstract

The paper outlines the research findings from a Library and Information Commission-funded project on the role of libraries and information services in supporting a learning society. The make-up of the team and objectives of the project are described.

The research was conducted by means of a series of case studies based on documentary analysis, formal and informal interviews and the use of observational data. This was carried out in five sites - a primary school, a further education college, a company, a hospital and a Learning City.

Illustrations and findings from the case studies are discussed. Conclusions are drawn regarding national provision of library resources, provision of technological resources, and partnerships between policy makers, practitioners and users. Issues of importance for future strategies are also highlighted.

Introduction

This paper will focus on a project that was supported by the Library and Information Commission on the role of libraries in the learning society. The project was identified as of importance to the Library and Information Commission before this had become a "sexy" topic as far as Government was concerned. From that point of view, it was a topic and a theme that pre-dated all of those discussions.

The task of the project team was to investigate the role of library and information services in supporting a learning society, and we took as our task the notion that we needed to bring together the questions and issues that are important within the library and information community, as well as those that are of importance to the academic community.

The project team reflected a combination of academic researchers on the one hand, but a professional librarian on the other. The professional librarian worked in tandem with the project team and on the final report, and she is credited as being one of the authors. It seemed to us very important that we should have professionals and researchers working together because it adds the dimension of realism to the kinds of questions that are posed.

We took as our starting point two statements. One was by Josh Hillman, who stated that if the interests of individuals coincided with those of employers and society as a whole, lifelong learning must start at school with a broad and solid foundation followed by recurrent and progressive periods of learning. And then, in turn, a statement in a Library and Information Commission report that stated:

> *"Tomorrow's new library will be a key agent in enabling people of all ages to prosper in the information society, helping them to acquire new skills for employment, use information creatively and improve the quality of their lives."*

Now these two statements seemed to us to be important in the course of framing a project on libraries and lifelong learning, and helped to shape our project objectives.

Objectives

The project objectives could be summarised as follows:- firstly, to demonstrate good practice and to provide evidence of the added value that libraries provide in supporting lifelong learning; and secondly, to examine the needs and experiences of learners in the context of age, libraries in the learning community and the purposes of learning. These seem to us to be the important areas that we should look at and helped frame some of our questions. These included such topics as "What is the role of the learner in the process of lifelong learning?", "What are the purposes of library use and how are these perceived by learners?", "How do library providers support education and training?", and "What kinds of partnerships are involved between libraries, institutions and other providers?". Now these questions, together with those two statements that I gave from the Library and Information Commission's report and from a document by Josh Hillman, helped to focus the project in terms of the kinds of work that we would be doing.

Research methods

We decided that if one is going to look at libraries in a learning society, it is important that you take a cross section of activities across society in order to pick up the use of library and information services at different points in people's careers. From that point of view, we decided that the most appropriate approach for this project was to conduct a series of case studies, and that the case studies would be based on a range of research strategies. Firstly, documentary analysis was used as in the library and information service, and we decided that the documents produced should be used as a key resource for the researchers. Secondly, the case studies would be based on a series of formal and informal interviews. Thirdly, they would be based on the use of observational data provided in situ. But in order to use these approaches, we needed to develop the project across five sites: a primary school; a further education college; a company; a hospital and a learning city. From that point of view, we saw the five case studies as providing data that would support the notion of how library and information services operate in terms of fulfilling the objectives of a learning society. It is all very well to talk in terms of the learning society, lifelong learning and the University for Industry, but they are actually concepts that have relatively little content and are rarely specified. One needs to begin to look at how these principles operate in practice in several case study sites. We deliberately decided that the case study sites should include a primary school library at one end of the spectrum through to the libraries outside the education service in a company and in a hospital. We were also interested in the range of library services that were provided in a learning city, so that one set of data cross checks the other. This is a very important strategy if you are going to have a study that will deliver both reliable and valid data.

Furthermore, it seemed to us that it was very important to see the extent to which different institutions and different organisations might be complementary in terms of the kinds of skills that were provided. It seems to me that if you are going to talk about enacting the notion of lifelong learning and the learning society, then we should not have to re-teach basic skills. Rather, we need to build on those skills in order that people can engage with ever-increasing levels of complexity and also derive a range of different activities and provision from libraries and information services on the basis of the knowledge and skills that they have acquired. Hence this particular range of case studies pick up those issues. In order to try and focus this a bit and to give a flavour of the report that has been published by the Library and Information Commission, we need to focus on one particular site. I want to take the further education college as an example, and to look at a site we called "Mounts Bay Further Education College", where the fieldwork and initial case study was conducted by Susan Band.

A case study of Mounts Bay Further Education College

Mounts Bay College is situated in a coastal area. It has five major sites for 16,000 students spanning an age range of 14 to 80, and there are 20,000 enrolments per year on the range of courses that are provided. Now in that context you have a spectrum of learning opportunities and learning engagements that one can study in order to see the way in which the principles of the learning society are enacted in practice, and the way in which the library situates itself within that. On the basis of an interview that Susan Band conducted with the College Principal, we felt that this quotation really sums up one of the key objectives of the College:

> "What lifelong learning means to me is creating the opportunities for individuals to access learning at different points in their lives and also at different levels. So I think my responsibility as College Principal is to try and make these opportunities available for the communities we serve through opening up the curriculum, creating learning centres, and creating a flexible curriculum which is modular-credit based."

However, if a college is going to be involved in opening up curricula, creating learning centres, and creating a flexible curriculum, then the role of the library, and its staff and the delivery of information is of paramount importance. Indeed, the way in which that is enacted is important in terms of thinking about how those demands have the potential to change the role of librarian and the role of the library within the College community. Certainly, one of the challenges of the learning society is not just to talk about those people who use the library service but also those people who work for the library service and to ask to what extent are library staff the agents of curriculum change and the agents of the learning society? If we are going to develop a knowledge-based society linked to the provision of a wide range of information services, then the role of library staff is critical in working in partnerships with other groups. Clearly within the further education college that meant working with teachers on the one hand and students on the other. Indeed it was our view that we needed to look at the role of the library service in the context of the institution, and to pick up the way in which the institution was developing effective practice through its library service and through sources of information and support. The role of the library was defined by one staff member who commented to us in interview:

> *"Whether it's library staff or the learning centre or learner support, we are all trying to offer a coherent support mechanism for all students and for staff as well."*

This emphasised the notion of building partnerships and building teams in order to provide a wide range of resources and materials. Indeed if you look at the College prospectus for this institution it reads as follows:

> *"We have students of all ages and from every walk of life and we especially welcome people who may be returning to study after a break and are nervous of taking the first step."*

Now that presents the challenge, not only for those who are delivering the curriculum in the classroom but also for library staff who are having to work in tandem with College teachers to provide an effective curriculum and an effective induction to further education. We saw there was a range of effective practice which supported lifelong learning in the wider community. Students were supported in their learning through learning centres, through learning resource co-ordinators who were multi-skilled in terms of library and information resources, and through opportunities for membership of the public library as well as the library service provided by the College. In order to get the delivery of the curriculum to be effective, we considered that it was very important to ensure that these different services complemented each other. This would result in the delivery of a multi-skilled individual who had sufficient library and information skills that could be taken into other venues. It is very important that alongside the formal curriculum, educational institutions actually provide user education through the library and information service. If people are going to maximise their opportunities in other areas of life, they require the services of different but complementary libraries. They may all be in the same physical location but the kind of service that they tap into will vary according to the kinds of demand that they are making of that service. One issue that we emphasised is the way in which a series of skills need to be developed in order that you do not end up with a situation where each time someone moves into a different location they have to almost re-learn basic skills. It calls for an integrated curriculum of user education across a range of different library and information services.

But what actually impedes the successful development of user education within this particular site? What were the barriers to success? Firstly, the role of technology.

We often underestimate whether we use technology or technology uses us. In this College, the demands for e-mail vastly outstretched the resources the institution had available. It is very important for us to begin to think about how we harness the use of technology, not least in terms of the costs involved. Secondly, there was still a demand for paper-based as well as computer-based resources, so how do you balance the level of resource between the different types of provision that the user demands? Thirdly, while we saw a wide range of facilities available, the question that one needs to think about in this institution, was the extent to which they complement each other and the extent to which usage could be rationalised. Certainly, as far as we were concerned, it was essential to examine the way in which the library, the service and the librarians needed to be proactive within an institution in order to help influence the policies on the curriculum and the policies that are enacted to bring about a learning society. Well, that gives a flavour of one of the institutions that we studied, but what general conclusions can be drawn from the overall study?

Conclusions

Firstly, with regard to resourcing, we feel that effective practice is dependent upon national provision, and we need to think about the kind of national provision that we have in this country. How do you complement the activities of the British Library on the one hand with the tiniest primary school library on the other? How can we convey to the public that the library is a massive national resource that we can all tap into?

Secondly, we need to think about the kinds of technological resources that are required if we are going to maintain the level and quality of service that we have. One of the things that many major reports underestimate is the massive reinvestment that is required with regard to technology. It is not a set of one-off purchases, it is a question of continuing renewal and we need to think about that. As far as libraries are concerned, we felt that there was a need to focus on the process of developing the information society as well as looking at the outcomes of the curriculum and learning that takes place. In that connection, we felt it was important to think about how one would develop indicators of performance with regard to library use and library provision. As far as librarians were concerned, we felt that the challenges of the learning society demonstrated that there was a need for librarians to be proactive and technologically-proficient, which meant that there would be training and retraining throughout their careers, and that should be a central component in the development of the library service. As far as users were concerned, it seemed that professional staff needed to give training in leading-edge developments if users were to make the best of the opportunities that are readily available. Without that we can have a superb library service nation-wide but, actually, the way in which individuals can access that library service might be somewhat curtailed, given their own lack of knowledge about leading-edge technological developments.

Finally, in thinking about the links between user education, the needs of the individual and the development of partnerships between libraries and those who provide lifelong learning in conjunction with the library service, there needs to be partnerships between policy makers, practitioners and users. Without that triangle being operative, it seems to me that we are not maximising the opportunities that we have, given the levels to which the principle of the learning age has been developed.

Future strategies

First of all, the library can be used to assist the transformation of education and training for learners. Unfortunately, it is the library community that is often told that it is a conservative force. However, we need to turn that round and say: "To what extent is it the users who are the conservative force?"; "How can the library community lift its profile to project a strong and vibrant image, and to demonstrate the potential for users if only they would utilise the opportunities?"

Secondly, there needs to be clarity on lifelong learning and the purpose and role of the library and information service. The concepts are interesting but until we start to develop some content around the concepts we will not be able to push this a long way forward.

Finally, we need to think about the way in which library partnerships and networks are developed with a range of other agencies. The networking of the library and information service with a variety of partners is of paramount importance.

The library: access and individual creativity

Professor Ernest Edmunds

Director of LUTCHI Research Centre
Loughborough University

Abstract

The paper argues that people learn best through activity and through interchange with others, and focuses on the role of individual creativity in learning. In particular, the creative use of computers is discussed, from early examples in creating music to more recent developments.

"Technology Foresight" is a Department of Trade and Industry programme looking at the ways in which technology will be important to the economy and quality of life in the UK in 10 or 12 years time. The issue of access is discussed and in particular questions about participation, level of interaction, genre, time scales and cost. Libraries are challenged to be fully involved in technologies for learning.

Introduction

I do not speak Russian but my Russian friends tell me that LUTCHI means 'best'. I come from the LUTCHI Research Centre and maybe that is good enough! To summarise, this is a research centre concerned with computer-human interaction. This last part, concerned with the impact of new technologies on people and in particular on how they use knowledge is most important. That is not really what I am going to talk about this afternoon and I perhaps would be allowed just to say that I use libraries and I am certainly in the learning community. I am a professor in a university but in other respects I am something of an outsider, and I will spend 20 minutes sharing with you some of the things that I have been involved with that hopefully might be of interest.

Active learning

The perspective which I would like to put to you is that we all learn best through activity and that active learning is something very important to us. Those of you – and there may not be so many – who remember the 1960s may remember that this perspective was quite normal then. We also learn very much through interchange with others, be they our peers, our teachers, or our students. I make that last point very strongly. As a professor my students teach me most. The point that I will focus on during my talk this afternoon is the role of individual creativity in the context of learning.

Creative learning

The word "creativity" is one that is very dear to my heart, and I believe is central to learning in any depth. I want to give you a bit of background here because I am concerned with the use of new technology, and lots of people think that the use of new technology is very dull and non-creative.

I want to go back to 1961. A little later than that, in the late 1960s, there was a film called *2001*. It was produced by Stanley Kubrick and written by Arthur C Clarke. There was a scene in it towards the end when Dave, one of the astronauts, tries to disconnect the computer, Hal, that is running the spacecraft, and as he does so, Hal begins to lose his mind. Hal describes how, when he was first constructed (there is an argument about which date he was first constructed in the story) he was taught to sing a song, "Daisy, Daisy, a bicycle made for two". Arthur C Clarke researched this and looked at the early usage of computers in ways that were creative, and he portrayed a number of instances in the film, including chess. In the previous example, Arthur C Clarke went to Bell Labs in the US, the place where a computer first sang a song. This was the first purely synthesised version of "Daisy, Daisy". There was no instrument involved it was all completed by a computer. That was 1961.

At that time it took very serious scientists with very serious computers to achieve this, and the unique thing that they did in 1961 that inspired Arthur C Clarke was to add a voice.

The point of this is that today we can buy software that can help to make this happen. It is quite normal to create music on computers today, even kids do it. Then it was very difficult. It was quite impressive for 1961.

Technology Foresight

I will now cover the core part, and I come at this from the Department of Trade and Industry's point of view. They are running a programme there called "Technology Foresight", which is trying to look into the future, some 20 years ahead, to see what technologies are going to be important for our economy and for our quality of life in the United Kingdom. A number of panels have been set up to look forward, and these have all sorts of worthy people on them. There is a panel called ITEC, which deals with Information Technology in Electronics Communications, and this has a sub-group concerned with creative media.

It is recognised that creative media, films, animation, music, electronic music, and so on are quite important in the UK economy. The problem from the UK economy point of view is that although we generate a lot of it, people elsewhere in the world make money out of it. It is also recognised that these creative media can be very important in terms of encouraging and enabling learning. The concept that computer games are terrible and people should be banned from using them, and that they should simply read a book to help them learn the most appropriate way, is simply not correct. It is no more correct than it is it to say that they should read books on screens rather than on paper. Actually, that is not what screens do best: paper is quite good for that kind of thing. Screens are good for other things and, as a matter of fact, the games makers have been prolific in generating good examples of what they can do, but with different objectives to most of us in this room.

Access and creativity

The creative media sub-group has formed six task groups and I chair one of them called Access and Creativity. We are concerned with providing access to the new technologies in order to enable people to be more creative in a broad context, and we have identified three important areas.

Firstly, access for artists in order for them to be more creative using the new technologies the cost of which is beyond the scope of their studios. In my University, well-known artists use hundreds of thousands of pounds worth of equipment which they cannot have in their studio but which they can use for a short time in between its use for other projects.

Secondly, there is specialist access for the people who know quite a lot about it - I think of this as the equivalent of the kids who formed a rock group. They know how to play guitars, they can make music, they are not stars but know a few things and can use a synthesiser. They actually have some expertise, but they do not have the facilities and all the expertise that they need. So there is room for helping and encouraging these people.

Thirdly, and relevant to this conference, is access to all this material. In my group, we have been looking at kinds of ways of providing access in a town – through the library, the working man's club, for example, the Labour Club. How can that access be provided in ways that relate to creative learning? We were very excited by the document *"Connecting the Learning Society: National Grid for Learning"*[1]. It is intended to provide the connections for information technology and access through libraries, schools, museums, colleges and so on. But my worry is that this will provide non creative access for information retrieval only, and that this will not actually achieve the objectives that we need. I have nothing against it in principle, but it may need something value-added so as to make it valuable to us, and that is what I most particularly would like to press this community to think about.

Dimensions of access

We have tried to look in some detail at what kinds of dimensions of access there might be. We came up with about 20 dimensions of access but we decided that there were some we would look at closely. They are these:

- participation - what kind of people are given access, who are they?

- interaction - what level of interaction is implied by this access? Is it completely passive, rather like watching a video, or is it like watching a television with one channel where you just watch whatever is provided, or is it like a video-on-demand where you at least choose what you watch? Or is it highly interactive like a lump of clay where you do whatever you want to do with it?

- genre - what kind of genre is it - music, film and so on?

- time scales - look at the initiatives in this country and abroad scheduled for delivery in 2001. Unless we deliver the content-based provision for creative access by 2001 we are in trouble because conservative forces will make it very hard to add what my group believes we should add.

- costs - when we talk about cost, we are not just talking cost to the Exchequer but society's total investment - my time, your time, children's time, everything.

Surveys of activities

We surveyed current activities and have been able to draw a graph of the kind of people that participate, against the level of interaction with a volume of activity. If you look at where effort is concentrated, for example, in educating children and adults, then you see that the educational activity is fairly busy in a particular area, and that educational institutions (university or college) rather than lifelong learning are involved. Activity is a little bit thin when it comes to kids and so on. I wanted to alert you to the fact that we are working on these kinds of activities and we are trying to map out what is going on and where the gaps are. This is an important area and we should also be trying to address the areas that should be included. This provides us with a way of making judgements.

We have visited media centres around the country and there are very good examples in Brighton and Huddersfield. These are operations that provide particular services in a particular environment which match some of the creative goals I have talked about. They provide information about access to information, for example across the Web. They provide information about activities that happen, such as people holding festivals across the Web, and have meetings and so on. They provide Internet access itself to casual users as well as planned sessions. There are cybercafés where you can buy a cup of coffee and have a sandwich or even have a glass of wine and sit at the computer and use the Internet. These environments are important in terms of providing an incentive to users. They also encourage micro-enterprises and small businesses to grow, and so they help the economy too.

The role of libraries

I would like to conclude by asking where the library is in this? When I became involved in this project, we travelled the country to all sorts of places, and we met all sorts of people, but we were surprised to find that media centres were being developed largely without much contact with libraries. I have not yet found one in a library. My challenge, I have to say from slightly outside the community, is what can the libraries do to provide all the rich and vast resources via this new media? They must go beyond the provision of information and they should provide for creative potential, creative learning and active learning for all their users.

Our last speaker pointed out that the key for the future is partnerships between agencies and I think my challenge can only be answered by appropriate partnerships because no agency, not even a library, can deal with everyone. May I remind you of the importance of creative use of these technologies for learning and of the engagement they offer people who are learning. The challenge is for libraries to be in there with that future or it will happen somewhere else.

References

1. Department for Education and Employment (DfEE). *Connecting the Learning Society: National Grid for Learning. The Government's Consultation Paper.* London: DfEE, 1997.

The role of libraries and information technology in the learning city

Sue Cara

Associate Director (Programmes and Policy)
NIACE

Abstract

Libraries have not been strong partners in the examples of learning cities in Britain, and it is crucial that they move to centre stage. The interrelated aims of learning cities are examined, including their role in supporting lifelong learning, in social and economic regeneration, and in the encouragement of personal development.

The key strands of learning city activity - partnership and planning, participation and performance - are then discussed with reference to libraries and ICT. The examining the challenge to libraries and the kinds of contribution they can make are examined.

Introduction

When I was asked to talk about the role of libraries and ICT in a learning city, I was in the middle of a project on learning cities. I had not heard a lot about the contribution of libraries in the initial phases, but I thought that would have changed by the time I came to carry out this task. Regrettably that has not been the case. In the learning city examples that I have looked at in Britain, libraries are not strong partners. In fact, you could say they were virtually invisible. I think moving from invisibility to centre stage is a fairly crucial and challenging task for libraries in terms of the kind of partnerships involved in learning city initiatives. I want look at learning cities and their focus. The information comes from a mapping study that I did for the DfEE last year, and a study that I have been doing this year which has been looking at the kind of "value-added" that learning city initiatives bring to communities. Then I want to look at the role of libraries and the challenges, of where libraries need to be in learning city initiatives. I want to start with what a learning city is.

What is a learning city?

Learning cities are about supporting lifelong learning, but they are also about social and economic regeneration. The way that libraries are generally regarded might be one reason why libraries are not thought of as the first automatic partner. Learning cities are interested in economic development and success. In particular, they are about economic regeneration, and the development of social cohesion, and the encouragement of personal development. Learning cities come from a European way of thinking, which is probably why they have not been embraced so energetically by cities in Britain. In the documents that inspired learning cities there were no British examples.

The idea is that local economies are different and that different places can make a difference by the way that they approach learning, and that learning is fundamental and important to the success of any local economy. There is a second strand which is about social cohesion - that communities are able to learn about themselves and learn how to make themselves better places to live, more creative, more successful, more pleasant to live in. Then there is a background theme about personal development: the skills that are involved in developing people, as people are also the skills that are needed both for communities and for the economy. Most learning cities have those three inter-related aims, and then they tend to have also some inter-related strands of activity.

Key strands of learning city activity

A strand around partnership and planning, so often the initial focus for the idea of the learning city, not surprisingly comes from the educational sector. But while the idea of the learning city is ghettoised in education, it has no chance of embracing the wider meaning of "lifelong". Once the education providers have sorted out their own kind of incoherence and difficulties they then think about a learning city. A real learning city moves outside the educational area alone and into other ways in which people engage in their community. So there is a double phase of partnership, an educational phase and a wider phase, in most of the examples in Britain. Then, because of the regeneration strand of interest, learning cities are also very interested in participation not just in learning but also in communities - in extending democracy, in people having a say in how their communities and their cities are developed.

The third strand focuses on performance. If Norwich decides that it will be a learning city and puts a good deal of energy into activities and partnership to promote that aim, and then markets itself as a learning city, it is not terribly useful or sensible unless it knows that it is doing better than the city next door which is quite happy to be an "ignorant city". There is an element of difficulty when you call yourself a learning city and you are bottom of every league table and you have not really done very well. The project I have recently been engaged in is looking at how you might measure the value that you have added by operating in a kind of partnership, in a collaborative way so as to increase the sum of learning that goes on, and whether that makes a successful and better place. So those three strands are there. But where does this leave libraries?

Libraries and ICT in partnership

When libraries have been involved in terms of partnerships in Britain, they tend to be on the fringes of the educational provider partnership. They are not centre stage, they are a resource added to what education providers are doing. There is a need for libraries to become major partners rather than relegated to the sidelines among the "other people consulted".

I think that libraries need to develop a vision of where they want to be in the learning city. Norwich is an exception really. As our library burnt down we are rather more keen on libraries than other places. We notice that we do not have a library and, because we might be building one, we tend to take it a bit more seriously, and so the library is actually considered as a central focus in things that are happening in Norwich and can be built into the strategy. In a lot of places, because the learning city is about building learning into the economic development strategy for the area, the library somehow gets left out. I think the challenge for libraries, libraries in all institutions and public libraries, is to build themselves a vision of where they want to be in terms of a learning city strategy.

There is a lot of talk and a lot of interest in ICT and the wired city and the wired town, but not a huge amount of actual practice. The rhetoric precedes the practice by quite a long way. If we are going to have a National Grid for Learning and we are going to be able to connect libraries (and I feel during this conference you will have thought about the way that information technology can be crucial to libraries far better than I can outline here), we also need to have the vision which enables libraries to be built into the strategy. Then the planning will follow.

Everybody involved in learning city initiatives needs to be concerned with the way that they will evaluate their contribution and to think about that at the beginning. Learning cities in the early stages tend to be about carrying out projects, rather than thinking about how well they have done or evaluating the value of what has happened.

Libraries, ICT and participation

The next strand of learning activities is about participation. As I have said, this is participation in a number ways, including learning. It will be very sad if libraries are not part of the UfI strategy for local learning centres. Local learning centres will not only need to be in libraries but also in the kind of places in the community which are not libraries and where people go. The trick will then be to think how those connect with more central resources like libraries and how those connections are made. How will learners be supported in those local learning centres either from a central resource like a library or in the centres, themselves? For NIACE, whose fundamental aim is to widen access to learning, local learning centres are the one way that people who do not have access to technology at work or at home may be able to develop some kind of equality or some kind of access to the kind of technologies they will need to engage in a learning society. Without that infrastructure, we were in danger of creating within our learning society, a more divided society than we have now. The idea of the local learning centre as an accessible, open and comfortable "place" for people to be is very important. Libraries are well placed to meet that kind of need. All the surveys of local services show that libraries, even if they are not used by all the population, are universally highly regarded and trusted by the population, and that puts them in a rather better place than a lot of other institutions when it comes to engaging with people who do not normally engage in education and training.

Libraries must also play a full part in the initiatives relating to economic progress and success. Libraries tend to be regarded as a kind of informal learning area and are valued for that, but when it comes to connecting employment, economic success and library services some of the links are not clearly made. There is job for libraries to do in improving such links.

Libraries already have a strong role as local information services, and that role will be an increasing one in learning cities. Certainly, the kind of exchange of information about community facilities within learning communities is a key one and I think libraries are well placed to take that role. I have talked about a kind of wired city. It is vital that libraries take a lead role in making it clear that those linkages can be made. One of the key strands in the participation work of learning cities is about engaging communities in planning their own futures - this is one area where it is important that libraries think about how they can engage better with local communities and local groups. Libraries have shown themselves to be really excellent in becoming involved in family learning and in supporting parents and children in their learning. They are less developed in the way that they might engage with other groups in the community. There is some interesting work to be done around developing links with other community groups. There are initiatives such as those in Birmingham and Liverpool, which are about giving individual community groups and neighbourhoods the power to purchase services, buy things in, and choose what they want. That is part of their engagement with the democratic process.

Libraries, ICT and performance

The last area I wish to look at is performance. Learning cities are rather keen on performance. As I said, they need to prove what they are doing, and libraries need to identify ways in which they might contribute to the value that is added by any kind of learning city initiative. Libraries are felt to be an important barometer of the level of informal learning that is going on in any community. Those counter figures and targets, which I am sure you will keep, are invaluable in getting a picture of the hub of activity that ought to be there in what is considered to be a learning city.

The definition of locally appropriate targets is a key one for learning cities. Local economies are different and local places are different, and if you are a learning city in Southampton, you do not have the same aims as the learning city in Sheffield. Locally appropriate targets are important. National reference points are also important because all the energy put into initiatives ought to produce better results within the community. They need to show they are not just better than the next place but at least moving up in terms of league tables and targets. A lot of attention is needed to the way that partnerships bring in additional output/input and benefits to the community. We need to look at whether a new learning centre on an estate really has changed things, whether there are more people coming into it, whether they are becoming better qualified, and whether they are moving on. These are the kinds of measurement that need to be built into any process and I suggest that libraries need to build them into their processes too, especially in new partnerships. Another way that people are using the idea of the learning city is to sell learning within the city. There are different strands to this. There are the kind of organisational structures which make a coherent infrastructure for learning, which is a good thing in terms of learning city initiatives. Because these are specifically around cities, one of the things they are able to do is to lean on people's sense of identity and where they come from. One of the ways that people have achieved this is to work with the media quite effectively to show different people learning and different kinds of situations in different kinds of places. We do not see enough of people learning through libraries and learning informally. The value of case studies of people who are learning in those ways is absolutely crucial in the marketing of learning.

Quite a few challenges. Learning cities are not the only examples of learning communities, and sometimes I do not think they are the best examples. They are just a collection of places that began to think about collaborative partnerships that preceded the Government saying collaborative partnerships are a good thing. Libraries could work with them but they can also work with other places equally well which have not taken on that label, so as to develop the infrastructure for a learning society.

Creating a setting for the learning city

Lawrence Revill

Director
David Lock Associates Ltd

Abstract

The author argues that, from a town planning and urban designer's view, as cities become more intelligent and the demand for information expands, people will become more insular. The city will respond by rediscovering the best settings for social interaction, and libraries can rediscover a central social role in that.

The paper goes on to consider libraries at the focus of social interaction, as both a social centre and a cultural centre, for example, Croydon Central Library and the Millennium Project in Durham.

The importance of rediscovering the city centre is emphasised, with reference to Ebbsfleet and Greater Brierley Hill, and the challenges of creating new communities with reference to Clyst Hayes in Devon.

The urban environment must increase in richness to support social interaction for the new learning communities of tomorrow.

Thesis

"As cities become more "intelligent" and the demand for information expands, the pressure will be for people to become more insular. But there is more to knowledge than simple information. The city will respond by rediscovering the best settings for social interaction. Libraries can rediscover a central social role."

I think I have been selected to make this presentation in order to open your eyes perhaps a little to some of the work that we do as town planners and urban design consultants, and the roles that we think libraries have to play in that. I would like to introduce David Lock Associates: we are town planning and urban design consultants, one of the leading practices in the country. We are involved primarily in large-scale regeneration and redevelopment projects but also in the design and development of new towns. We are not necessarily just about buildings, infrastructure and roads but as much about creating new communities and, therefore, about people and the things that people actually need to live their lives.

My thesis is the following: that as cities become more intelligent and the demand for information expands, the pressure will be for people to become more insular; but there is more to knowledge than simple information. The city will respond by rediscovering the best settings for social interaction, and libraries can rediscover a central social role in that. Put simply, as people are learning to become more independent, to find more of their enjoyment in information at home, there is a pressure on all of us to create cities which are rich places where people can find lots of locations where they can get together, and that is one of the underlying themes behind my practice's work. This is revealed in lots of new thinking and new places.

My first example is a company that I used to work for, DEGW International. They are architects and space planners and leading edge consultants in the design of the work place. They create the workplace as a club and in their own plan for their own workplace they have created something which is a microcosm of how towns should be, in that it is a very rich environment. People do not necessarily have their own workstation - they come in and pick up a phone and put their computer on a desk and plug it in to the nearest socket. Alongside that there are all sorts of other places, such as the area which is called the club. It has soft chairs and tables for people to have informal meetings, to meet one another and to exchange information. It has coffee points at which people meet as well as informal and formal meeting rooms. It also has an area known as the archive which is where they store all their product information and which is effectively the library for this community. This is one way of thinking about the workplace which is starting to change the conventional norm, from people sitting at a desk all day and not really necessarily having much to do with their work mates, to a place which is actually facilitating people talking to each other and is very much a learning community.

On a much larger scale, British Airways are in the process of building a new corporate headquarters near Heathrow Airport. They have created a series of buildings linked by a street that has all the characteristics that you would expect of a street. It has cafés, shops, and a library and information centre as part of that network, around which are distinctive office buildings relating to that street. It is the place where there is lots of informal communication between people, again creating a learning community.

Libraries at the focus of social interaction

Libraries at the focus of this social interaction are something in which I am very interested. That idea of the library as a club, a place where people actually choose to go to meet other people, is very important to my mind, but so is the library as a cultural centre. There have, historically, been many libraries attached to art galleries and museums and many are being developed with a cultural emphasis as part of their core facilities. They are even associated with more commercial cultural activities and commercial galleries where products are for sale and not just to be viewed. However, there is also the library as an entertainment centre. There are libraries now which have cinemas within them, or house cybercafés where entertainment is as much the product they are delivering as education or information. All these elements contribute to the social focus of libraries. A particularly good example is Croydon Central Library which was redeveloped a few years ago to create exactly that. The library, the collection of information, is still the core facility, but it does have galleries, bookshops, cafés and cinemas as part of that overall scheme.

We are dealing with something that is on a slightly different scale, a smaller scale, in the redevelopment of Ipswich Airport in Suffolk, where we are putting together a proposal for a new resource centre as part of the development. It is a development of a thousand houses on the site of Ipswich Airport, in a deprived and disadvantaged community in the surrounding area. It also includes a new primary school and we intend to try and attach to that a branch library, a village hall, and a computer resources centre. All these facilities together are intended to provide for the primary school children and their learning requirements; to provide facilities for home-workers and home-learners and give them access to better information facilities; to create a facility after school for a homework club for secondary school children who find it difficult to study at home or to get hold of information at home; for the general public; and to facilitate adult education in the evenings and at weekends. This is a relatively small facility, but nevertheless it is right at the core of that development project.

Libraries at the focus of cultural interaction

In Durham, we have been engaged to look at a master plan for the redevelopment of a large amount of land through the heart of Durham, land which is currently lying vacant. The Millennium Project includes a new central library facility, the centre for learning at the top of the hill alongside the Millennium Hall, and a commercial cinema development as part of that site. It includes a mixed-use development of housing, cafés, shops and bars, with car parking facilities for this whole complex. It also includes a new pub and restaurant and other facilities, new housing along by the river and a new river bridge connecting to other new facilities on the other side. The library is very much at the core of the whole raft of new developments which will enliven and enrich that particular environment.

On a much greater scale, we are involved in a project to create a new city centre in the heart of existing communities on the south banks of the River Thames in North Kent. Ebosfleet is the core, and is intended to be the location of a new international passenger railway station on the Channel Tunnel Rail Link when, or if, that ever comes to pass. It sits between Gravesend and Gravesham, with the Dartford community: and the town of Dartford, on the other side. This is very much a mixed-use development it has living, working, shopping and leisure as a cohesive development in the centre of the site. The new railway link runs through the heart of the development with a new station, and then some high-density, high-quality urban development around it, providing a shopping, residential and leisure environment in a very strong landscape setting, but with very good connections to all of the existing communities. Libraries might be located in a logical and rational position within the overall plan so as to make sure that they are as accessible as they can be to the maximum number of people they are intended to serve, and certainly there is provision within the plan for a major new central library facility for the whole of the North Kent community. As well as the existing population of about 250,000 there will be 45,000 new homes and 70,000 new jobs created over the next 25 years. It is a very large scale of development.

Rediscovering the city centre

A slightly different case study is that of what we have now called Greater Brierley Hill in the West Midlands, better known as Merry Hill, where the major shopping centre is. At the moment it has the reputation of having destroyed the town centres around it by focusing all the shopping in one place. There are leisure facilities attached but it is mainly shopping. We have been given the challenge of creating a new community, increasing the amount of shopping floor space but in effect creating a new town centre for the whole area. At the heart of it will be a new civic focus adjoining the main shopping area which will contain a sports stadium, new offices for the Council, new commercial offices - all the things that you would expect to find in a town centre - in which library and information facilities and education facilities will play a major part. The idea is to turn it into a much more sustainable community too and to actually provide those facilities in places which are accessible to people, where they do not necessarily have to rely on their cars to get to. They can use public transport much more easily but people will also be able to walk more easily and find a good, high-quality pedestrian environment which will link them into the new facilities around them.

Creating new communities

My final example is the idea of creating new communities at a place called Clyst Hayes in Devon, immediately adjacent to Exeter airport. We are designing and planning a new town for approximately 18,000 people with potentially 4,500 to 5,000 new homes and the jobs and facilities that go along with that, on a greenfield site. There is not a community here at the moment and it is to address the need for new housing development in the whole of Devon that this particular location has been selected. The master plan itself involves Exeter airport and a substantial new employment development, but the main area of development is a new mixed-use residential community with employment facilities and accommodation built into it, but with a new town centre as part of that which will be easily accessible. No point in the town is more than ten minutes' walk from any other part of the community. The public transport facilities are very well developed as part of the plan but a substantial number of the residential community will actually be within five minutes walk of the town centre, meaning that all those facilities which are required are within easy access of every home. It is building communities where accessibility is a fundamental principle, and is starting to address this issue of creating opportunities for social interaction in which libraries in particular, but lots of other facilities in general, will play a major part.

Conclusion

As life becomes more insular, so the urban environment must increase in richness to support social interaction. Hopefully, people will once again rediscover the positive aspects of urban life. I think we have all become used to suburban life and the fact that everything is disjointed, and everything you need to do requires you to get into a car and to travel long distances to do it. This discourages people from meeting other people on a very regular basis, though it is the way of life that we have all become used to. What we are trying to get back to is recognising the qualities of urban life in some of the planning work that we are doing and creating new social foci for people to actually meet, including reinvented libraries of the sort that we have been hearing about in this conference. I have become much more certain over the last couple of days that new and reinvented library facilities will be very much in the vanguard of providing those core opportunities for social interaction that the new communities of tomorrow will require.

Creating a learning society

Professor Nick Moore

Senior Partner
Acumen UK

Abstract

The paper argues that we are at the beginning of a period of profound social, economic and cultural change, and there is a need for society to change to correspond to that.

The key principles required for this are to move form information to knowledge, to move from a position of technological determination to one of social embeddedness, and to move from developments based on markets towards a situation where development is driven by what is socially desirable.

In order to make these moves and create a learning society, the paper argues that there are three steps. Firstly, we need to change the social contexts within which we live, secondly to change the ways in which organisations work, and thirdly, to build and actively support the knowledge sector of the economy, both private and public.

The paper maintains that there is leadership and commitment already in different parts of the education sector, and in the library sector, but these must be brought together if we are to create a learning society.

Introduction

We are living at the beginning of a period of profound social, economic, cultural and political change. We need to change our society: its structure, shape, purpose, and function, in order to correspond to that. The need is not restricted to Britain, it is common to all countries in the developed world and increasingly, to many countries in the developing world. We cannot escape those pressures, and the need to change. If we simply ignore it then we will consign ourselves to a backwater that will be difficult to leave.

Key principles for change

We have to face the challenges ahead and do it robustly and enthusiastically, and we must try to do two things. We must try to maximise the opportunities that are opening up and will increasingly open up to us. We must try to minimise the undesirable effects of the consequences that will also come a long with those changes. In doing this, we should be guided by a number of key principles. Two of them, the first two, I would take from the European Commission's high-level expert group on the Information Society. (This is recommended reading. It is an extremely good rationalisation and justification for the sorts of changes we are talking about.) They identify two key principles. First, we should move from information to knowledge. We should aim to develop, in their words, a wise society, a society in which skills and knowledge are applied so that information is used for the greater social good. This is about much more than just information it is the application of knowledge. We should also, they argue, move from a position of technological determinism to one of social embeddedness. Terrible jargon terms (I am sure it has suffered in translation) but I think what they mean is that we should reject the notion that our world is shaped and dominated by technology. It is true, they argue, that technology shapes society. It is also true however, that society can be used to shape technology. We have the power, we have the opportunity, we have the scope within us to shape the course of technological development so that it corresponds to and benefits the society in which we live, and I believe we must take that power, we must assert that power. To those two principles, I would add a third, which is also important in the context of the thinking within the European Commission and perhaps within the thinking in British Government. We must move from developments that are based on markets, that are driven by market forces, towards a situation where development is driven by what is socially desirable. We must reject in particular the propositions put forward by Commissioner Martin Bangemann and the European Commission that market forces hold the key to the development of an information society and the direction which that development should take. If you are in any doubt about this read the article in the latest issue of *"Information Strategy"* where he asserts that market forces are going to be the sole driver of development of an information society in Europe. This is very frightening. We need to recognise the breadth of the arena occupied by the public sector in this whole area of development. What we should aim to do is to harness the technology, make that shift from information to knowledge, we should aim to develop a society based on what is socially desirable in order to create a learning society.

Steps in creating a learning society

There are three steps that need to be taken to facilitate this. First, we need to change the social contexts within which we live: the social, cultural, and political worlds that we occupy. Secondly, we need to change the way organisations work. We need to move and develop our organisational base to one which implies a much more information-and knowledge-intensive style of operation and, as part of this, will need to shift our focus of attention from a concern with productivity to a concern with "value-added". We need to build and actively support the knowledge sector of the economy in the widest terms. The private and public part of that knowledge sector needs development. It will be the source of our future wealth creation and an essential means of satisfying, developing and meeting the demand that will fuel our future economic growth and development.

Consider the first of those, changing the social context. What is needed to create a society which supports learning, which supports all the objectives of a socially inclusive society, and which recognises the value of the investment in learning? Think back to Bob Fryer's frightening statistic. Few of the people in the categories he was talking about have any concept of investing in their learning ability and probably very little belief that any such investment will produce a worthwhile return. This is a bit of a problem. Efforts are based on the supply side of the equation. The National Grid for Learning, the New Library Network, the University for Industry, all seem to be predicated on an assumption that once the supply mechanism is in place there will be demands to respond to it. Is this a valid assumption? What is needed is a programme of action to stimulate the demand for learning. This needs to focus very definitely on the socially excluded. Ways of bringing them back into the learning mainstream for the first time need to be identified.

We need to create a society that encourages cultural enrichment in the widest possible sense. Think of Kate Adie talking about the burning down of Sarajevo library. People said to her that after the library was destroyed, life was becoming coarser. How many of you feel that life in Britain is not becoming coarser, as time goes on? We face very powerful forces that are lowering the tone of our cultural life within Britain. The power of mass popular culture, the power of the lowest common denominator, and the power of Rupert Murdoch. We face the cultural hegemony of Hollywood, a situation where so much of our culture is created by an industry which has massive economies of scale and which benefits the United States, partly because of the English language but mostly because it has such a huge home market. The power of global communications and the power of that set of economic circumstances puts cultures all over the world in grave jeopardy. We need to guard and take active action against this. We are in a good position to do that: just as we have powerful forces lowering the tone of our cultural life so we have powerful forces that can be used to prop it up, to support it, to strengthen it, and to enrich it. We have probably the best public service broadcasting system in the world although it is under consistent attack from all areas. The UK has probably one of the best publishing systems in the world although, one which increasingly owned, with a few very notable exceptions, by large American conglomerates. There is a wonderful film industry, Lord Puttnam is a classic example, and yet the biggest problem that British film producers and directors experience is releasing their films in British cinemas because the screens are linked to American dominated film distribution systems. There are excellent theatres and public libraries. There are museums, art galleries and so on. They need to be fostered and nurtured to re-create a culture that is enriching. We need to create a knowledgeable and accountable democracy. This is a sound-bite political culture. Alistair Campbell is going before a Select Committee of the House of Commons today to defend the present Government's approach towards its media relations. The present Government is really no different from the Governments that have gone before. There is a system where more and more political information with a large P and a small p is provided and yet there is less and less understanding. There is a professed system of open government and a steady increase in the degree of media manipulation. All this is happening at a time when political issues are growing in complexity and that requires a degree of informed-ness, knowledge, mass participation and awareness. We need better political education from a much earlier age.

There is a need for a change in the way organisations work. There are two challenges. All organisations should be smarter. They should be better able to use the knowledge and the information they have at their disposal. We should encourage a shift to more knowledge-rich activity as a whole within the economy. The whole economic system is dominated by a concern with productivity. The basic challenge is production for less. Low price becomes the main selling point leading to low cost production, which in turn does not encourage investment in intelligent working or human capital. If we consider value-added instead, then we have a very different set of rules to work to. If the question was not how can we produce for less, but how can more value be added, then value for money is emphasised rather than low price. This change in emphasis will encourage investment, particularly in people. People need to be engaged with the organisations in which they work.

Again, Bob Fryer quoted that statistically 86% or so of the working population have not received any training or learning opportunities in the preceding three months. How, if intelligent knowledge-intensive work is to be encouraged, can there be long-term survival? Can we expect any degree of commitment from people who work in that sort of barren environment? How many organisations actively encourage and stimulate creative thinking? How many of them are tolerant of failure? How many of them are fun to work in? Work ought to be fun! To give commitment to an organisation, you need to think about what is needed, what you are doing, and approach your work from a knowledgeable point of view. To do this there should be enjoyment in the process of work.

We need to support generally the whole process of learning and self-development. The training and learning gap in organisations should be seriously addressed. There is a very real excitement about the New Opportunities Fund for training public libraries in information technology. It is a positive step forward and something that has been waiting to happen for so long but it equates to £767.43 per worker employed in the public library. That is nothing for training people in a knowledge-intensive organisation and yet we are so pleased with this little amount and are sure it can be used to lever further resources, but we need to start thinking in a much, much bigger way about training people and developing their intellectual ability. We need to build and take more steps to support the creation of the knowledge sector in the economy. This is an essential driver of future economic growth and wealth creation. It will be required to satisfy the internally-generated demand for information and knowledge, but it will also be important in terms of our future development and training position in global markets. It will be the knowledge sector of the economy that will add most value and wealth and compete most vigorously in international markets in the future. There is a need to channel and make the most of market forces. This is a very powerful sector. There is a lot of money at stake, and a very powerful force driving the issues. We are extremely well placed in global markets: ironically the British film industry is much more successful overseas than it is in this country. We have an amazingly successful export-layered publishing industry. British librarians are in demand all over the world as consultants for World Bank and for other agencies. We are very, very well placed to take advantage of those global markets. What we need is a sound regulatory framework within which all that market-layered activity can take place. It should also be recognised, however, that the public sector is a powerful driver.

The public sector alone is a major information provider. The creator of learning products in the learning society will always take account of market failure and this is biggest in dealing with and addressing the learning needs of the socially excluded. In building the knowledge sector of the economy, equal weight should be given to the development of the public sector.

A strategic framework is required. This is essential to bring about change. A clear vision, unity of purpose and a sense of momentum are all required. Sadly, I feel that all three of these are lacking in Britain at the moment. If we compare ourselves to our partners and competitors overseas, they are very well endowed and have clear vision statements on the whole. Partners from member states within the European Community have very clear vision statements about the information and learning society they want to create. They have frameworks of policies, backed by actions to put the information society in place. These programmes of actions and policies are backed at the very highest level. The vision in general was produced by committees chaired by Prime Ministers of the relevant country. They also have significant levels of public sector investment leading to high levels of private sector investment that is beginning to pay dividends in terms of improved services, greater levels of participation and slow but steady reductions in social exclusion. What can the UK provide in comparison? There is *"The Information Age"*, the vision statement produced by the Prime Minister which seems to have sunk almost without trace. It needs much more vigorous promotion to have any effect. Again, we should be grateful for it, the first statement of its kind, but it is little more than a post-op rationalisation of many things already in place. The statement should be a primary example of joined-up thinking within Government, but just like the wig that Ernie Wise used to wear, you can see the joins between the different chapters. There is very little inter-relationship, no mechanism for co-ordinating the work of the Government's departments in the future, and no mechanism for keeping the vision statement up to date. There is no sense that the information or learning society we are creating in Britain is part of the emergence of a wider society within the European Union. There is a paucity of investment. We must be grateful for and respect the amount of money the present Government is providing for *"The People's Library Network"*, but the cost estimate by the Library and Information Commission was much higher than the sums of money being made available now.

There is an outdated concept of the role of private finance in the whole process of developing the information society. If we are going to build a public library network, we ought to pay for it out of public funds and yet we have the idea that private investment is good and public investment is bad whereas, in reality the differences are relatively small. There is no real sense of leadership or commitment in any of the areas within the education or library sectors. The Library and Information Commission is, I believe, doing a powerful job in raising the level of libraries and the role that they can play in the future, particularly within government circles. In each of the little boxes, things are happening, but nobody is bringing those boxes together and providing the commitment. We can continue to muddle along in what we think of as our comfortable British way but the reality is that all the time we are slipping further and further back in the field. Taking the analogy of *"Chariots of Fire"*, if we carry on like that after another couple of laps around the track we will be out of reach of the leaders. If we are serious about creating a learning society, then it is about time we got our act together.

Strategic partnerships for lifelong learning: how libraries must change

Professor Peter Brophy

Director of the Centre for Research in Library & Information Management
(CERLIM)
Manchester Metropolitan University

Abstract

In this paper, the results of a major study into the impact of lifelong learning on academic libraries are described. A definition of lifelong learning is offered, and the impacts of information and communications technologies are outlined. Government policy initiatives are summarised and a number of relevant academic library initiatives described. The conclusions of the study are then given in detail, ranging from the need to ensure that suitable basic services for lifelong learners are in place to the need to improve academic librarians' expertise in the development of new, electronic services on which innovative approaches can be built.

Introduction

During the last two years the Centre for Research in Library & Information Management, now at the Manchester Metropolitan University, has been conducting a study into the future impacts of lifelong learning on higher education libraries. Funded under the Electronic Libraries Programme (eLib), a major report on this work has recently been published under the title "*The Development of UK Academic Library Services in the Context of Lifelong Learning.*"[1]

Background

Our approach to the task of forecasting likely future changes and their impact on academic libraries was to:

- examine what is meant by *lifelong learning* both through analysis of the published literature and through examination of Government announcements and policy statements

- study the concept of *learning* with particular reference to its higher education context, in order to ground our understanding in the realities of one of the most basic issues, 'How do students learn?'

- take particular note of the impacts of Information and Communications Technologies (ICTs)

- examine in detail recent major reviews, including the Dearing Report (officially the Report of the National Committee of Inquiry into Higher Education),[2] the Kennedy Report,[3] the Fryer Report[4] and the major Government Green Paper "*The Learning Age*"[5]

- examine case studies of academic libraries which had developed services targeted especially at the needs of lifelong learners, particularly at mature learners and those studying at a distance

- develop a series of 13 conclusions and 23 recommendations addressed to the funding bodies, to institutions, to library managers and to the librarianship profession

Lifelong learning

After considerable debate we decided that we needed to develop our own definition of lifelong learning, with emphases as set out below:

> *Lifelong learning is a deliberate progression throughout the life of an individual, where the initial acquisition of knowledge and skills is*

reviewed and *upgraded* *continuously*, *to meet* *challenges* *set by an ever changing* *society*.

By using this definition we hoped to draw attention to a number of salient features of lifelong learning, namely:

- it relies on a deliberate decision by an individual to pursue learning. Although we all learn from life all the time, the term lifelong learning implies that there is a decision to pursue learning in order to acquire new knowledge and/or skills

- it continues throughout life, so that a series of learning activities are undertaken, and it is never supposed that learning is complete or that new learning cannot be undertaken

- there is a process of review so that the experience of earlier learning occasions (whether successful or not) is subjected to careful consideration, with gaps and new opportunities identified

- a process of updating is undertaken, so that skills and knowledge acquired earlier in life are brought up to date and made current in the light of developments in knowledge and changes in society

- the updating of knowledge and skills is seen as a continuous activity, such that they are not allowed to become seriously out of date or irrelevant to current concerns and practices

- individuals are open to the challenges to their knowledge and skills which changes in their own lives, and in society, present, and they use learning opportunities to respond to those challenges

- it is accepted that society is in a constant state of change, and lifelong learning is one of the main agencies through which individuals can respond to and cope with that change. Conversely, it is accepted that society itself needs individual members to learn new skills and knowledge if it is to remain viable and prosper in an increasingly competitive world

Information and communications technologies

In conducting our research we were very aware that one of the major issues for educators today is the harnessing of the opportunities provided by information and communications Technologies (ICTs). There is a great deal of hype around the potential of ICTs to "revolutionise" learning, and it is sometimes forgotten that learning is, at heart, a social activity – so many of the skills we need in the modern world are those of working with others: communicating effectively, working in teams, co-ordinating the knowledge of different specialists, and so on. As yet, we do not know just how revolutionary ICTs will prove to be. What we do know is that they can make a tremendous contribution to effective learning. From the primary school to the university, ICTs provide the means for effective use of multimedia, for interactive group working, for co-operative studies involving international partnerships and for much more. The electronic content of the World Wide Web, with all its drawbacks and limitations, has made massive impacts on the ways that information can be accessed in support of learning. Whether or not the changes brought about by the application of ICTs are revolutionary, they are certainly massive.

In our report, therefore, we examined developments in multimedia, computer-mediated communications, the electronic library, networked learner support, and the TLTP programme. Each of these has the potential to change the way in which learning is carried out, and each impacts on the development of the academic library in different ways. As such they provide a backdrop to discussions on lifelong learning.

The policy framework

A major part of the report was concerned with setting out the framework for current interest in lifelong learning. This framework has been long in the making. We examined reports from the European Commission which culminated in the designation of 1996 as the European Year of Lifelong Learning. As Edith Cresson, EC Commissioner for Education, Training and Youth, remarked, the need is for all citizens to be "encouraged and empowered to take on more responsibility for planning and carrying through their own personal and professional development on a lifelong basis".[6]

In the UK too, lifelong learning policy has had a considerable gestation. It is not the invention of the current Government, but can be traced back through the activities of organisations like the Workers' Educational Association, the extra-mural work of universities and even to early nineteenth century initiatives like the foundation in industrial towns of the Mechanics' Institutes. In more recent years, policy papers like the former Conservative Government's consultative paper on lifetime learning[7] published in 1996 which focused on continuing education and training, and the updating of skills beyond the initial education phase, i.e. schools, colleges, universities. The paper looked towards the role of employers and how government can contribute to developing the culture of lifetime learning and stressed the importance of "a highly motivated, flexible and well qualified workforce to the United Kingdom's international competitiveness".

Lifelong learning has reached the top of the UK's political agenda through a series of policy papers and reports published since the new Government took office in May 1997. In our study we examined in detail – and abstracted the key issues for library development – the Dearing, Kennedy and Fryer Reports and the Green Paper, *"The Learning Age"* being the primary sources. We looked also at *"New Library: the People's Network"* and at the National Grid for Learning proposals. One of the interesting issues to emerge from this analysis was the growing recognition – by non-librarians! – of the contribution that libraries have to make. One quotation from the Fryer Report will illustrate this:

> *"In promoting lifelong learning, and widening access, full use should be made of the major community resource which is invested in libraries, museums and study centres. They already have an excellent track record in providing learners of all ages and from a variety of backgrounds with a rich and diverse range of materials, opportunities, information, facilities and staff support. They need to be seen more widely as part of a mosaic of both local and national provision, offering additional arena through which the culture of lifelong learning for all can be fostered and sustained. They too need to be connected to the proposed National Grid for Learning and their staff should be supported in developing further the skills and aptitudes which will be necessary to carry through the new strategy."*

In addition to Government policy documents, we spent some time examining other, related initiatives. We were particularly concerned to point to the Royal Society of Arts' Campaign for Learning[8] with its emphasis on the "messiness" of learning and the need for each individual to be encouraged to find their own learning style and model. The Campaign for Learning also emphasises the need to adopt an iterative model of the following kind:

- create a safe environment – and so enhance motivation

- remove self-limiting beliefs - ranging from "Show me and then leave me to it" to "I can't do that" - learning can be painful as well as rewarding

- identify individual learning styles - encourage learners to consider their learning strengths and weaknesses

- identify positive outcomes - manageable/achievable/relevant goals or "chunks"

- identify the steps needed to achieve these outcomes – create a learning plan

- take those steps - include application/practice. Much of what we learn is adapting to new challenges - learning environments need to be constantly re-evaluated

- review progress regularly – provide feedback and support from mentors and teachers – and allow flexibility for changes

- achieve results - build confidence/self esteem - learn from mistakes in a blame-free culture (the "safe environment" again)

- start again

Libraries and lifelong learning

Our analysis of current library initiatives to support lifelong learning illustrated that, although there are excellent initiatives in all library sectors, including the academic sector which was the primary focus of our work, there is little co-ordinated effort and learners are very often left to negotiate library facilities for themselves. Interesting background research includes the work on franchising undertaken by Brophy and Goodall, [9] studies on library support for distance learning at Sheffield University[10] and of course the cross-sectoral initiatives here at Sunderland.

In addition there are interesting developments taking place in the development of new operational services. The Open University is launching new electronic services, including the ROUTES (Resources for Open University Teachers and Students) system which is building up a database of learning support materials available online. At Thames Valley University, the Learning Resource Centre is a flexible, one-stop-shop learning facility, open 24 hours a day, seven days a week, designed with non-traditional, lifelong learners in mind. Electronic library facilities will play an important role in the University of the Highlands and Islands Project,[11] which aims to develop a new university which will offer students in the remoter areas of Scotland the opportunity to undertake a growing number of higher education courses on a full or part-time basis which can be attended at a specific college or at a remote location. Students who are studying on franchised courses run by the University of Central Lancashire[12] are able to use the services of the Virtual Academic Library of the North West (VALNOW) service which was launched in 1997, and is described in a separate paper at this conference. Sheffield Hallam University offers students a Distance Learning Support Service[13] with a range of services to off-campus students. The service offers distance learning support to students studying on courses that have been deemed as appropriate to distance learning. As well as sending out books and articles in the post to students, the service also offers book loans for up to three weeks, an interlibrary loan service and photocopying and supply of journal articles.

In addition to these academic library examples, we looked briefly at what is happening in the public library sector, and at the impact of co-operative initiatives such as the Consortium of Academic Libraries in Manchester (CALIM) and the London-based "M25" Group. Even where such developments have not been motivated primarily by the needs of lifelong learners, they offer an important strand of development for non-traditional learners and particularly those based at a distance from their "home" institution.

Research conclusions

Our report concluded with 13 conclusions and 23 recommendations, the latter directed at the Funding Councils, the institutions, librarians and the professional associations. The recommendations will be found in the Report itself, and ranged from:

> *"There should be continued encouragement at the highest level for co-operative approaches to comprehensive library provision suitable for supporting lifelong learners. In particular, given the likelihood of courses of any one institution being followed by students across the UK and any one student following modules from more than one institution, there is a need to go beyond regional arrangements and consider the issue again from a national perspective."*

to:

> *"Institutions should ensure that when they offer courses designed to appeal to lifelong learners, and especially where those courses will not be delivered primarily on-campus, there is a clear statement of the learning resource, including library, support which will be available and a commitment to its delivery. Work is needed to develop understanding of the costs and benefits of library support in these contexts."*

Our conclusions can be stated in full. They demonstrate that the effects of the new lifelong learning agenda on higher education libraries will be extensive, and that considerable efforts are needed to achieve a culture change within which the needs of non-traditional lifelong learners are given equal weight with those of traditional students.

We therefore concluded that:

- higher education libraries will need to commit themselves to develop, publicise and deliver a *basic set of library services designed for lifelong learners*. As Dearing found, it is the basic, "bread and butter" services such as access to books and study space that learners themselves regard as the highest priority. Redesigning service delivery to account for the needs of lifelong learners is thus a very high priority

- on the other hand, libraries need to refocus their services on *content* rather than form, and ask themselves how the required content can be delivered to the lifelong learner – rather than becoming blocked by the difficulties particular forms present. Here they can provide leadership in how information sources can be presented within the structures of learning which teaching staff devise

- the *hybrid library* concept has much to offer the lifelong learner through its emphasis on a managed mix of traditional and electronic services. Current *e*Lib hybrid library and clump projects should be encouraged to take on board the needs of lifelong learners if they have not already done so

- *convergence* should be seen as a positive step for the lifelong learner, since it provides a single point of contact for academic support services and ensures that a single policy is pursued in their interests

- the future of library support for higher education lifelong learners will best be secured through *multi-agency provision*, by which is meant a planned and managed co-operative alliance of providers (university, further education, public etc. libraries and others). However, because courses will be marketed nationally and internationally, it will not be adequate to rely only on regional co-operation

- a key issue will be the extent of *integration of library services into learning*. As new learning environments are designed and established the role of the library will change - what is being introduced is an entirely new kind of environment where the student can easily and within the same interface access information ("library") and expertise ("tutor") while discussing ideas with fellow students ("seminar") and using a self-diagnostic tool

- libraries will continue to play their sometimes unrecognised role as *social centres*. They are places where people can meet, study in groups as well as individually, and find supportive experts. For the off-campus lifelong learner, this role might be found in the public or college library, but will only be satisfactory where it is planned, resourced and managed with lifelong learners in mind

- *information quality* will be a matter of increasing importance since electronic services are often not subject to the level of quality control exercised over printed and other traditional publications. Libraries have an important role to play in quality assurance, and again lifelong learners will need this support, especially where their study is unmediated and off-campus

- *electronic resources* offer new and exciting opportunities for supporting lifelong learners with the information they need. However we lack, as a library community, good models of the electronic library in its world-wide networked setting. We also, as a profession, lack the depth of knowledge that is needed to design and create the electronic services of the future

- *information skills* pose a particular problem for the lifelong learner, who is typically short of time and may be remote from the physical library with its expert advisers. Where, as Dearing recommended, skills work is embedded in the curriculum librarians will have to redouble their efforts to ensure that information skills are adequately covered and assessed

- for the non-traditional, lifelong learner the provision of good *helpdesk services* may make the difference between success and failure. However, these services need to be designed as part of the overall learning environment, so that academic staff are involved in and take account of their design and function, and the help desk is not the last, desperate port of call

- if lifelong learning is to be a reality, universities will need to think in terms of developing *lifelong relationships* with their clientele. Libraries, through their "external" and other membership arrangements, could be in the vanguard of this movement

- finally, the rate of change is so rapid and the agenda to be addressed so vast that academic libraries will need *dynamic management* if they are to serve the needs of lifelong learners

Conclusion

The research reported here provided a comprehensive analysis of the current environment of lifelong learning development, a thorough review of academic library responses and a set of recommendations and conclusions pointing up where various actions were needed by different agencies. It is likely that CERLIM will continue its research in this field and will be monitoring the impacts of the major Government-led initiatives in this area over the next few years. In so doing we welcome opportunities to collaborate with other researchers in this field, and likewise opportunities to discuss our work further with those involved in the design and delivery of services. Interested delegates can contact the CERLIM research team at cerlim@mmu.ac.uk

References

1. Brophy, P., Craven, J. and Fisher, S.M. *The development of UK academic library services in the context of lifelong learning* London: Library Information Technology Centre on behalf of JISC, 1998. Also available at http://www.ukoln.ac.uk/

2. The National Committee of Inquiry into Higher Education. *Higher Education in the Learning Society*: Report of the National Committee (Chairman: Sir Ron Dearing) London: HMSO, 1997.

3. *Learning works: Widening participation in Further Education* (Chairman: Helena Kennedy, QC) Coventry: Further Education Funding Council, 1997.

4. Fryer, R.H. *Learning for the twenty-first century*: First Report of the National Advisory Group for Continuing Education and Lifelong Learning, 1997.

5. *The Learning Age* http://www.lifelonglearning.co.uk/greenpaper/index.htm

6. Reported in Giere, U. *Lifelong learners in the literature: adventurers, artists, dreamers, old wise men, technologists, unemployed, little witches and yuppies*, International Review of Education. 40, no. 3 - 5, 1994, pp.383 - 393.

7. Secretaries of State for Education and Employment, *Lifetime learning: a consultation document*. 1996. http://transcend.co.uk/LIFELONG_LEARNING.CONSULT.CHATITLE.htm, 1996.

8. Greany, Toby, *Reaching our potential in a learning society: the Campaign for Learning assesses how we can learn to learn*, RSA Journal, CXLV, no.5479, May, 1997, pp.8-9.

9. Goodall, D. and Brophy, P. *A comparable experience? library support for franchised courses in higher education.* (British Library Research and Innovation Report: 33) University of Central Lancashire, 1997

10. Unwin, L., Bolton, N. and Stephens, K. *The role of the library in distance learning: implications for policy and practice.* Library and Information Briefings (6), May 1995

11. University of The Highlands and Islands Project: November 1995 *Submission to The Millennium Commission.* Highlands and Islands Enterprise, 1995. See also http://www.uhi.ac.uk

12. University of Central Lancashire http://www.uclan.ac.uk

13. Sheffield Hallam University Learning Centre's Distance Learner Support Service: http://www.shu.ac.uk/services/lc/

Concluding remarks

Matthew Evans CBE

Chairman, Library and Information Commission
Chairman, Faber & Faber Ltd

I arrived yesterday morning and travelled up with Tessa Blackstone and David Puttnam, and we were met by Andrew McDonald. No sooner had we got into the car than Andrew said, "Let me tell you, Lady Blackstone, about our wonderful library system," and for the half-hour journey from Newcastle to Sunderland he talked about libraries. Every time there was a pause Andrew again said, "Look at this public library... let me tell you about this... let me tell you about that...". This was an absolutely great start to the conference, because Tessa was able to hear how important libraries are, and I am very grateful to Andrew for that.

I think we have to ask what is the value of these conferences. I came up with four ideas and perhaps other people will have more:

- there is a chance for people to discuss ideas

- a chance to sow the seeds of ideas and concepts that may bear fruit later on

- I think perhaps most important of all, identifying emerging themes, however painful they are. (I think some very tough and very justifiable questions have been asked over the last two days about the place of the public library system, its relationship with other organisations, where is it going and even whether there is an actual role for public librarians in this new future.)

- if a conference can attract the attention of people who have real political power, this is a great benefit. I wouldn't say this in other contexts but I do think that within the library context this is very important.

When I became Chairman of the Commission three years ago, one of the things I noted immediately was there was no group of people of influence or political power speaking out for libraries. In publishing we have such a group, and in television there is a most wonderful and effective pressure group. This is an issue of great importance and I think that by attracting Baroness Blackstone and Lord Puttnam here, we have put ourselves in a position of developing such a powerful group for libraries.

One of the themes of the conference has been the need for strategic partnerships to help libraries, particularly public libraries facing major change. Libraries cannot stand alone - they must have partnerships with other organisations to survive. However, when we talk about strategic partnerships, we must include partnerships with people, as I think these are as important as with organisations. For example, I was able to talk to Tessa Blackstone about how libraries could support the University for Industry, and she said that she would ensure that the University for Industry was indeed delivered into the public library system. That is the sort of thing that demonstrates how important these partnerships with people of influence can be.

Similarly, it is wonderful that David Puttnam has played such a key role in this conference. I think what emerged yesterday in discussions with him is that he is genuinely keen and interested in the future of our library system. Melvyn Bragg, who has just been ennobled, is also a great supporter of libraries, and I am sure that Melvyn would join with these baronesses and peers to help us through what is going to be a challenging time.

This morning we broke into three groups and there were three very interesting discussions going on simultaneously. I have in front of me notes from the three meetings and under the three headings there were:

1.   what are the benefits of strategic partnerships?

2.   what are the key factors for successful partnerships?

3.   what are the barriers to strategic partnerships?

I would just like to pick out a couple from each.

Firstly, no-one is saying we should not have strategic partnerships. Under the benefits, one of the eight things listed is that the whole is greater than the sum of the parts. If only everyone concerned with libraries, lifelong learning, and every manifestation of the Government's educational policy could actually move together in harmony to the common end, the sum of the whole would certainly be greater than the sum of the parts.

Secondly, what are the key factors for successful partnerships? The first thing here is to share a vision. We will only make progress if there is a constructive cross-sectoral approach for the benefit of all of us. In the shared vision we must not forget the private sector. My own view is that the library system will not survive unless it embraces the private sector. It is the relationship between this great public service and the private sector that is going to be one of the challenges for you to work out over the next few years.

What are the barriers? I have added two to the list of about twelve that emerged this morning. One is a lack of coordination between the various information initiatives from Government departments. There are some wonderful opportunities for libraries to play key roles in delivering these initiatives but, without coordination between them, the library world, and I suspect many other worlds, are going to find it immensely difficult to move forward without unnecessary duplication and fragmentation of effort.

The other thing I think we ought to keep very much in mind is the international perspective. We have had two days talking about libraries in the UK, but we are now living in a global society, and our libraries' relationship with libraries and information services in other countries is of paramount importance. There is also a danger that, if we are too inward looking, we will not embrace all the cultures from these other countries that so enrich our own.

I was particularly interested in the contributions this afternoon, because in one way or another, while the public library system was not being criticised, it was being suggested that an enormous amount of work has to be done to re-position it, and I think that is a message we should all take away.

I would like in conclusion to thank a number of people. This conference has been about partnerships and I think has demonstrated a very successful partnership between the Library and Information Commission and the University of Sunderland. It is the Commission's first conference and we are particularly grateful to the University of Sunderland for doing it with us. We will learn things from it and I think that it has been both interesting and a success. I would like to thank Anne Wright, the Vice-Chancellor, David Puttnam who is the Chancellor of the University and the planning group from the Library and Information Commission and the University of Sunderland, which was headed by Margaret Haines and Andrew McDonald. The support staff have been absolutely wonderful - many of them have been outside helping and making sure that we all go to the right place on time and I also have to thank, as was mentioned last night by Anne, the sponsors and the exhibitors. Finally, the chairs and speakers who have done an absolutely terrific job. I am not a librarian and my boredom threshold on the library world is pretty low, but I have found the whole thing absolutely fascinating. So thank you speakers, and thank you chairs.

Finally, thank you. It was very good of you to come and I would like in particular to thank those who have travelled from abroad. The international perspective is of enormous importance and it is wonderful to see you here. If I may, I would just like to pick out one person whom I have met before and was absolutely delighted to see here again and that is Councillor Sid Henderson who is the chair of Libraries and Arts at Gateshead Council. It is so wonderful to meet an elected official who is actually going to make the decisions about everything we talk about, and it is such a great pity that we cannot seem to get more elected members to these conferences. I had a very good talk with Sid in Durham and it is a great pleasure to see him here representing elected members. So thank you very much indeed.

Summary of discussion points from case studies

Group discussions were held after the case studies when each group considered the following questions:

- What are the *benefits* of strategic partnerships?

- What are the *key factors* for successful partnerships?

- What are the *barriers* for strategic partnerships?

What are the benefits of strategic partnerships?

We need to be clear that the ultimate beneficiaries should be the users, the general public, lifelong learners, rather than the libraries. But by working together through strategic partnerships, the whole will be greater than the sum of the parts. In other words, libraries of all types have a huge role to play in creating learning communities but our role and contribution can be greatly enhanced by working together for the benefit of the users of our services.

We can share expertise and resources and avoid "reinventing the wheel". In particular, training is an area where expertise and skills could be shared. Expertise, in particular areas, can be exploited by a much wider group of users.

We can increase access to a wider range of information than would normally be the case. More users can benefit from access to information from a different site or sector, or through partnerships, we may be able to make joint purchases of services that would not be cost-effective for one partner alone. Indeed, cost sharing is an important benefit, allowing partners to achieve aims they could not achieve alone. Improving services for learning communities is the real challenge but considerable economies of scale may also be possible.

Partnerships can bring considerable benefits for the profile and status of the partners and we can exert greater influence and increase the impact of information and culture for learning. Strategic partnerships could help maintain our independence in a competitive world, and our competitive position in relation to large corporations. They will also effect ownership by the learning community and improve contact with parts of the community not easily reached before (the have-nots).

Partnerships could well have beneficial effects in encouraging all the partners, and generating energy and greater participation. They can raise awareness of new possibilities and approaches, and expand horizons for each partner through the sharing of ideas, knowledge and skills.

Indeed, some participants felt that partnerships are vital - we have no choice! More must be done to reinforce those that already exist and to change our culture where necessary in order to facilitate partnerships and develop new ones.

What are the key factors for successful partnerships?

We need a shared vision and a positive culture which embraces library services to learners in the next century, and we need to foster cross-sectoral partnerships. A clear focus and mission are needed, based on continuing local consultation.

There must be a commitment to change among the partners. Library staff require enhanced and additional skills, for example, influencing skills, assertiveness, IT skills, facilitating skills. Individuals are needed who think globally, act locally.

Reinforcing good practice, progress and sustainability is important, and the larger institutions should ensure this. Information sharing across the partnership is essential. There is also a need for regular evaluation, including evaluation of our roles and performance in lifelong learning.

Partnerships should make an impact on people. We must discover how to reach those who most need the services, and how to show people the benefits of lifelong learning for them in jobs, the local economy, improving literacy and so on. The aim should be to achieve a measure of community ownership.

Communication and promotion of learning are important. We need to make it as attractive and useful as possible (infotainment).

It may be necessary to look for new sources of funding. As we enter a period of 'fiscal conservatism', how do we persuade taxpayers to invest in libraries?

New areas for partnership must be actively considered, for example, schools, the health sector, the voluntary sector, the business community and, from the private sector, computing, telecoms, the book trade and publishing.

What are the barriers to strategic partnerships?

A lack of "joined-up" thinking within and between sectors and departments, and competition between the organisations involved, can all create considerable barriers. There are differences in culture, agendas, funding and timescales.

A number of problems arise over funding. First and foremost, there is a lack of funding in the UK for partnership activities. We need to have public money made available, or make the concept more attractive to the private sector, or both. This is particularly important for sustainability. It may be necessary to look at priorities and the reallocation of funds.

There is a need for much greater development of the IT skills and technical expertise required for successful delivery of electronic information, and to build up networks and communication between partners. Costs can also be prohibitive in this area, for example the high costs of network licences, and the limiting of some licences, by sector.

The skills base of users is crucial in facilitating access to the full range of information available. For example, low levels of literacy can prevent the aims of the partnership from being properly achieved.

Participants discussed the image of libraries and librarians. A poor image can be a barrier between libraries and their communities, as can any tendency to be an 'ivory tower' or to be overly cautious (hiding our light under a bushel).

There is the question about how we can best serve the business community, especially SME's, and whether limited public library opening hours are a major constraint.

Contributors

Baroness Blackstone
Minister of State, Department for Education and Employment

Baroness Blackstone was educated at Ware Grammar School and the London School of Economics.

She became a Life Peer in 1987 and since then has been Opposition Spokeswoman in the Lords for Education and Science (1988-92); Treasury (1990-91); Trade and Industry (1992-97) and Principal Opposition spokesman for foreign affairs (1992-97).

Between 1966 and 1975, Baroness Blackstone was a lecturer at the LSE and during the Wilson and Callaghan Governments she worked in the Central Policy Review Staff. She was subsequently Professor of Educational Administration at the Institute of Education and then the Deputy Education Officer at the ILEA. From 1987-91, she was Chairman of the BBC's General Advisory Council.

In 1987, Baroness Blackstone was appointed Master of Birkbeck.

Her personal interests include ballet, cinema, opera, tennis and walking. Baroness Blackstone has two grown up children and three grandchildren.

Professor Peter Brophy
Department of Information & Communications,
Manchester Metropolitan University

Professor of Information Management and Director of the Centre for Research in Library & Information Management (CERLIM), Manchester Metropolitan University. Directed the Electronic Libraries Programme's Supporting Study on "The Impact of Lifelong Learning in UK Academic Libraries". Formerly University Librarian, University of Central Lancashire.

Professor Robert Burgess
Pro Vice-Chancellor and Director of CEDAR, University of Warwick

Robert Burgess is Pro Vice-Chancellor and Director of CEDAR (Centre for Educational Development, Appraisal and Research) and Professor of Sociology at the University of Warwick. His main teaching and research interests are in social research methodology; qualitative methods and the sociology of education; the study of schools, classrooms and curricula. He has written ethnographic studies of secondary schools and is currently working on case studies of schools and higher education. His main publications include; *Experiencing comprehensive education* (1983), *In the field: an introduction to field research* (1984), *Education, schools and schooling* (1985), *Sociology education and schools* (1986), *Schools at work* (1988 with Rosemary Deem), *Implementing in-service education and training* (1993 with John Connor, Sheila Galloway, Marlene Morrison and Malcolm Newton), and *Research methods* (1993), together with over twenty edited volumes on qualitative methods and education. He was recently President of the British Sociological Association and is currently President of the Association for the Teaching of the Social Sciences and founding Chairman of the UK Council for Graduate Education. He is currently a member of the Council and Chair of the Postgraduate Training Board of the Economic and Social Research Council.

Sue Cara
Associate Director (Programmes and Policy), NIACE

Sue Cara is the Associate Director (Programmes and Policy), at NIACE (The National Organisation for Adult Learning), responsible for leading the Conferences and Publications Teams for the administrative arrangements of the organisation. In addition, Sue has a particular lead role in relation to adult learning in Local Authorities. Prior to working at NIACE, she was the Principal Adult Education Officer for Norfolk running a directly delivered service with over 30,000 students involved in both FEFC funded and non-accredited programmes. Since being at NIACE she has carried out project work for the BBC, HEFC and for the DfEE, the latter in connection with the development of Learning City Initiatives in Britain. Sue has been a board member of the Further Education Development Agency, is also a member of the FEFC's Consultative Group on External Institutions and has recently served on the DfEE's Further Education Student Support Advisory Group.

Conn Crawford
Senior Policy Officer (Information Society), City of Sunderland

Conn is a secondee to City of Sunderland Council from the Northern Informatics (Regional) Partnership, with the task of helping to move forward the City's internationally recognised "Telematics Strategy", and in particular plans for a City-wide municipal network - the "Wheel of Opportunity". An Irishman, he has been working in the North-East since 1982, and offers a background in community-led local economic development initiatives developed with local authority support.

John Dolan
Head of Central Library, Birmingham

John Dolan is the Head of Central Library in Birmingham - "probably" the biggest and busiest public library in Europe serving the City's population of one million people and with a large regional audience too. In addition he is responsible for research and performance in Birmingham Library Services and is currently leading a long-term plan for the development of the Central Library.

In 1997 he worked as Project Leader to the Library & Information Commission's working group on public library networking which produced the widely acclaimed report, *"New Library: The People's Network"*.

The recent Government response to this report is the basis for current planning on the further development of public library networking. As part of this process John is chairing the LIC's Content Creation Task Group which will draft guideline proposals on the exploitation of the Lottery funding for lifelong learning resources.

John Dolan previously worked in St. Helens, Merseyside and for Manchester City libraries.

Professor Ernest Edmonds
Director of LUTCHI Research Centre, Loughborough University

Ernest Edmonds is Professor of Computer Studies at Loughborough University and Executive Director of LUTCHI (Loughborough University Telecommunications and Computer-Human Interaction Research Centre).

Professor Edmonds founded and developed LUTCHI, which is concerned with Computer-Human Interaction and, in particular, with human creativity using computers. He has conducted research in the area of computing in art and design for more than 25 years, and has more than 150 publications to his name.

He Chairs the Creativity & Cognition series of International Meetings. He is also Chair of the DTI's Technology Foresight Creative Media Task Group.

Matthew Evans CBE
Chairman of the Library and Information Commission
Chairman of Faber & Faber Ltd

In 1964, after one year in the bookselling trade, Matthew Evans joined Faber and Faber Ltd. He was Managing Director from 1972 until 1993 and has been Chairman since 1981.

Matthew was also a Council Member of the Publishers Association from 1978 to 1984 and in this role led missions to India and Pakistan to discuss copyright matters and initiated the idea of the Book Marketing Council to expand the market for books in the UK.

He has also been Chairman of the National Book League and the English Stage Company and Deputy Chairman of the British Film Institute. He is a founder member of the Groucho Club and was a Director from 1982 to 1997.

Currently, Matthew is Chairman of Festival Radio and a member of a number of national committees including the DCMS Advisory Panel for Public Appointments, the Arts Council National Lottery Advisory Panel, the University for Industry Advisory Group and Sir Richard Eyre's Working Group on the Royal Opera House. He is also a Fellow of the Royal Society of Arts.

Matthew has been Chairman of the Library and Information Commission since 1995 and was the Chair of the Working Group which produced *"New Library: the People's Network"* in 1997. He is currently chairing a new committee which is responding to Government with further advice on the implementation of a UK public library network.

Matthew received a CBE for services to Librarianship and Information Provision in the 1998 Queens' Birthday Honours List.

Professor Bob Fryer
Chair of National Advisory Group for Continuing Education
and Lifelong Learning

Professor Bob Fryer is Principal and Chief Executive of the Northern College and the first holder of the Bill Owen Chair of Continuing Education at Sheffield Hallam University. He has been Principal of the Northern College since September 1983.

Bob worked at Warwick University from 1971 - 1983 where he was first a Research Fellow in industrial relations and became a Senior Lecturer in sociology and the

Head of Sociology Department and the Chair of Faculty of Social Studies (the largest faculty in the University). He was a member of the University Steering Committee, the most Senior Management Committee in the University of Warwick.

During his time at Warwick (1971 - 1983) Bob undertook a series of studies for, and on behalf of, trade unions which were undergoing major structural and organisational change and responding to changes in the labour market and work organisation. Two were path-breaking studies of change in unions and led to substantial union reorganisation. Subsequently, Bob undertook similar work for a wide range of trade unions culminating in being the senior academic advisor in the merger between the three public services unions, NALGO, NUPE and COHSE.

Bob has provided consultancy and advice in a broad field of employment to government departments, employers, employers' organisations, trade unions and individual companies. He has written widely on employment matters including changes in labour markets, in training and education and in respect of organisational change and development. His current concerns have to do with the impact of increased competitiveness and globalisation on the changing employment structure of the UK and the role that education and training can perform in helping individuals and communities adapt to those changes.

More recently, in May 1997, he was appointed Chair of the Government's National Advisory Group for continuing Education and Lifelong Learning.

Hilary Hammond
Acting Director of Cultural Services, Norfolk County Council

Hilary Hammond was educated at North Western Polytechnic, London. He has worked as Luton Music Librarian; Leicestershire Group Librarian; Assistant County Librarian, Shropshire; Assistant Director of Libraries and Information in Suffolk; Director of Arts and Libraries in Norfolk and currently Acting Director of Cultural Services in Norfolk.

Ineke Herweijer
Councillor of City of Utrecht, Netherlands

Ineke Herweijer has a MA in French and Law and has worked as a teacher and Project manager for the International Association of Railway Companies. Since 1978 Ineke Herweijer was elected member of several local and regional councils. She was Deputy Mayor of Utrecht for the last four years and is President of TeleRegions Network, a European Association of regions involved in ICT projects.

Millard Johnson
Executive Director, INCOLSA

Millard Johnson is Executive Director of the Indiana Co-operative Library Services Authority (INCOLSA). INCOLSA is Indiana's library network consisting of more than 740 institutional members from school, public, academic and special libraries.

Mr Johnson holds a BSc. degree in experimental psychology and M.L.S. in library science, both from the University of Washington. He is a graduate of a post master's year in library automation at Washington University in St Louis sponsored by the National Library of Medicine.

Most of his professional career has been in computing and systems design in medical libraries. Before coming to Indiana to take the position of Executive Director of INCOLSA in November 1995, Mr Johnson was Director of Network Development at PORTALS - consortia of 14 academic and research libraries in Portland, Oregon.

Professor Andrew McDonald
Director of Information Services, University of Sunderland

Andrew McDonald is Director of Information Services at the University of Sunderland and Professor of Information Management and Strategy. His previous position was Deputy Librarian at Newcastle University.

At Sunderland, he has led the development of library and information services which includes new self-services, extensive electronic services, service standards, services for distance learners and innovative buildings. Unique cross-sectoral partnerships have been developed with the broader library and information community in Sunderland to meet the needs of lifelong learners in the City. He is closely involved in the University for Industry Pilot Project at the University and the City Partnership's *Telematics Strategy*.

He is chair of the Academic & Research Libraries Committee of the Library Association and sits on Council. A member of SCONUL's Executive Board, he also chairs its Advisory Committee on Buildings.

He has published widely and has contributed to conferences on library planning and design, quality management, digital library development and lifelong learning. He has directed several International Seminars for the British Council for whom he has undertaken consultancy projects all over the world. Research interests include lifelong learning, digital libraries and information skills training with grants from the British Library Research and Innovation Centre and the EC.

Professor Nick Moore
Senior Partner, Acumen UK

Professor Nick Moore established Acumen in 1983 to explore a wide range of issues concerned with the use of information in society. Since then, he has undertaken a substantial programme of research, consultancy and policy analysis assignments in Britain, Europe and overseas.

During the 1980s, his work at Acumen focused on two main issues: the changing nature and structure of the information workforce and the development of techniques for measuring the performance of libraries and information services. More recently his work has been concerned with the analysis of policies supporting the development of information societies and the application of information and communication technology to improve the performance of government.

Nick Moore was appointed the first Professor of Information Management at Birmingham Polytechnic in 1987. In 1989 he joined the Policy Studies Institute to establish a programme of information policy research. During this period he developed a series of studies into the European information content industry. In 1995-6 he was associated with the British Council, studying the development of information societies in East Asia and advising the Council on its information strategy in that region. In 1998 he re-joined Acumen to continue his research and consultancy.

He is a part-time Professor in the Department of Information Science at City University and a Visiting Fellow of Bristol University.

Nick Moore has presented numerous conference papers all over the world and has published widely.

Ian Pigott
Principal Administrator, European Commission

Born and educated in Newcastle upon Tyne, after five years in Canada working mainly as a translator, Mr Pigott joined the European Commission in 1973 where he headed the Systran machine translation development. He has worked in the libraries sector for the past five years where he has been involved in project management and Web site support.

Lord Puttnam of Queensgate CBE
Chancellor, University of Sunderland, Chairman, Enigma Productions Ltd

World renowned film maker Lord Puttnam of Queensgate CBE became the first Chancellor of the University of Sunderland in 1997. He has achieved great distinction in the film industry as one of its most highly regarded producers. His long-standing association with higher education and training led to his appointment to the Department for Education and Employment's Standards Task Force, and to the Government's Creative Industries Taskforce. He is a Visiting Professor and a Governor of the London School of Economics, holds honorary doctorates from a number of British universities, and is a strong supporter of lifelong learning initiatives, such as University for Industry, and innovative global teaching and learning involving new technology.

On his appointment as Chancellor, Lord Puttnam said: "I could not be more pleased... I am entirely in sympathy with the approach to higher education being pioneered at Sunderland and I am particularly excited to be able to play a small role in the future of this remarkable institution".

Lawrence Revill
Director, David Lock Associates Ltd

Town planner and urban designer. Consultant with one of the UK's leading planning and urban design consultants since 1993. Previously Associate Director with DEGW International working in the UK and across Europe. Specialist in large-scale development and regeneration projects.

David Ruddick
Technical Resources Institute, the Gates Library Foundation

David Ruddick graduated with a BA in English and spent a year teaching high school English. He received a Masters degree from the University of Washington's Graduate School of Library and Information Science and worked for the Seattle Public Library in the Centre for Technology.

David is currently the Network Engineer for the Technology Resource Institute, the Gates Library Foundation where he has helped to build public computing labs in high schools, colleges and public libraries across the country. His latest project is working with the state of Louisiana to help build a state-wide network providing connectivity to sixty parish library systems. His specialities include networking and network security in the public environment.

Dr Anne Wright CBE DL
Vice-Chancellor & Chief Executive, University of Sunderland

Dr Anne Wright has been Vice-Chancellor of the University of Sunderland since the institution gained University status in 1992. She had been appointed as Rector and Chief Executive of the former Sunderland Polytechnic in 1990. Dr Wright was appointed CBE for Services to Higher Education in the New Year's Honours List 1997.

Dr Wright has also been appointed to the Equal Opportunities Commission and is a member of the Opportunity 2000 National Target Team. She is also a member of the National Advisory Council on Education and Training Targets.

The Vice-Chancellor plays a leading role in the Sunderland community and holds several key posts.

Since Dr Wright's appointment at Sunderland, student numbers have grown from 7,000 to 15,000 and she has overseen the development of the award-winning St Peter's Campus on the Riverside.

Abbreviations

ALSA	Area Library Service Authorities
CALIM	Consortium of Academic Libraries in Manchester
CERLIM	Centre for Research in Library and Information Management
DCMS	Department for Culture, Media and Sport
EARL	Electronic Access to Resources in Libraries
HyLiFe	Hybrid Library of the Future
ICT	Information and Communications Technology
IT	Information Technology
INCOLSA	Indiana Co-operative Library Services Authority
INSPIRE	Virtual Library Network of Indiana
ISDN	Integrated Services Digital network
ITEC	Information Technology in Electronics Communications
JANET	Joint Academic Network
JISC	Joint Information Systems Committee
LASH	Libraries Access Sunderland Scheme
LSTA	Library Service and Technology Appropriation
LUTCHI	Loughborough University Telecommunications and Computer-Human Interaction Council
NIACE	National Organisation for Adult Learning
OECD	Organisation for Economic Co-operation and Development

OPAC	Online Public Access Catalogue
SCONUL	Standing Conference of National and University Libraries
TLTP	Teaching and Learning Technology Programme
UfI	University for Industry
UNESCO	United Nations Educational, Scientific and Cultural Organisation
VALNOW	Virtual Academic Library of the North West
WOW	Windows On the World

Index